Dionicio Morales:
A Life in Two Cultures

by

Dionicio Morales

PIÑATA BOOKS
HOUSTON, TEXAS
1997

This volume is made possible through grants from the National Endowment for the Arts (a federal agency), Andrew W. Mellon Foundation, the Lila Wallace-Reader's Digest Fund and the City of Houston through The Cultural Arts Council of Houston, Harris County.

Piñata Books are full of surprises!

Piñata Books
A Division of Arte Público Press
University of Houston
Houston, Texas 77204-2090

Cover art by Ignacio Gomez
Cover design by Mark Piñón

Morales, Dionicio.
    Dionicio Morales : a life in two cultures / by Dionicio Morales.
        p.   cm.
    Includes bibliographical references.
    ISBN 1-55885-211-5 (pbk. : alk. paper)
    1. Morales, Dionicio. 2. Mexican Americans-- Biography.   3. Political activists--United States--Biography.   4. Mexican American Opportunity Foundation--History.   5. Mexican Americans--California--Ventura County--Social conditions.   6. Ventura County (Calif.)--Biography. I. Title.
E184.M5m66   1997
973'.046872073—dc21   97-22160
                                                    CIP

The paper used in this publication meets the requirements of the American National Standard for Permanence of Paper for Printed Library Materials Z39.48-1984. ∞

Dionicio Morales:
A Life in Two Cultures

Dedication

To My Granddaughter, Amor Padilla Morales

Amor was the shining star of my life—a blessing to all our family and an inspiration to everyone who knew her.

In her brief life, her irrepressible youth had already sensed the cosmic verities. She dreamed above and beyond the shifting sands of mundane time and culture.

She brightened the groves of academe at the foot of the San Gabriel Mountains, just as confidently as she soared, with the sureness of an eagle, to editorial distinction in the shadow of Orizaba. She personified the realization of my dreams.

To all of us whose hearts she touched and transformed, her radiant spirit lives.

Acknowledgements

It is difficult to find adequate words to express my appreciation for the diligence, devotion and patience of a friend who has shared with me the endless hours we spent on the preparation of this manuscript. He painstakingly deciphered my notes, listened to my tapes, recorded my dictation and assisted my research. But, all of this was but a continuation of five decades of association.

In my lifetime, I have come to know many non-Mexican Americans who have achieved great understanding of our culture; but I have met none that I would compare in compassion for our barrio life and in faith in our future, to William H. Hensey, Jr.

A special word of appreciation goes to creative consultant, researcher and writer, Jose de la Islas III of Houston, Texas, who assisted in verifying and putting together the early historical data I required.

To the late Amor Padilla Morales, my granddaughter, goes my everlasting appreciation. She devoted many hours to authenticating all references to Mexico in my manuscript. Amor's outstanding talent in journalism first manifested itself when she was editor of Pasadena City College's student newspaper, *The Courier*. The college honored her with an opportunity to study for a semester at Oxford. Upon graduation from college, she moved to Mexico City, where she became a copy editor for the Mexico City News and became known for her interest in hemispheric relations. She had lived for the day of my book's publication. But on June 23, 1996, she suffered a fatal accident in Mexico City.

⌀

To East Los Angeles' feature writer-columnist, Rose Marie Soto, with whom I shared many hours of illuminating dialogue about East Los Angeles life, I feel profound gratitude and appreciation.

⌀

To the erudite enlightenment and personal encouragement of the eminent Professor David Hayes-Bautista of the University of California at Los Angeles, I attribute my broadened perspective on current and rapidly changing socio-economic realities of East Los Angeles.

⌀

To my dear friend, Fernando Oaxaca, with whom I have worked many years. We collaborated on .the Rebuild L. A. project. He provided me with valuable insights into the need for inclusion of our people in the destiny of Los Angeles. For this, I offer my profound respect and gratitude.

Introduction

The story of my life is not really much different from that of any other Mexican American who was young in the 20s and 30s. Except for specific details, mine is the story of many of our people—and it is meant to be. In retrospect, those experiences which occurred in my life and in the lives of my contemporaries seem to be repeating themselves even in the present generation.

For those whose lives can be seen in mine, this is an opportunity for them to share comparable experiences and memories. For those who have never known that such a world existed, here is an opportunity for them to discover and understand how and why some of us were molded by our lives to fight, others to accept defeat and still others, who could have done much, but chose the path of silent resignation.

When I think about the people and events that have helped shape my life, I realize the degree to which my destiny was part of history. Long before I entered this world, a rich and vibrant culture created by my forefathers and inherited by my parents awaited me. My future as an American citizen was sealed on the day my parents, like so many others, decided to flee the decade of turbulence that shook Mexico during the Revolution of 1910.

I entered a new world as my parents left theirs behind forever. Little could I foresee that in doing so, I was to become a person of two rich cultures, but a person perceived by some to be a "stranger" in both lands. All that mattered at the time was that I was blessed by birth to be the child of Narcisa Arenas and Severo Morales.

The story of my parents' flight north and my birth in their chosen refuge, the United States, seems to have presaged my entire career—ever on the edge, daring to take on something untried, always discovering new things.

Like most of my friends, I have been fascinated with the valiant story of our people's unrelenting struggle in search of a better life. This interest has kept me tied to my roots and reinforced my desire to be a strong, confident American citizen while remaining linked to the world our parents left behind.

In my work with the neglected poor, I have become painfully aware that so much valuable time has been consumed in conferences, redundant studies and endless rhetoric regarding the real-life challenges facing our people. I have noticed the multitude of books written about us by self-appointed experts who are not Mexican Americans. Too many of these have been, to me, a totally unnecessary burden to our cause. Such often irrelevant literature frequently turns out to be empty words instead of action.

I have always been a believer in rolling up my sleeves and facing any given situation squarely, rather than just talking. Action, immediate and decisive, has continued to be my watchword and it has been difficult for me to resist showing the scorn I have felt toward those who merely criticize or boast.

Yet, I have written a book, the story of my life. The words herein tell the saga of more than sixty active years, years of more pain than victory. It is also a history about achieving my lifelong objective: the institutionalization of basic human services, the result of which became one of the largest Mexican American human service institutions in the United States—the Mexican American Opportunity Foundation.

El Bajío: My Mexican Roots

Had my mother arrived in the United States two weeks later than she did, I would have been born in Mexico. But my citizenship was determined when she entered the country over the hot sands of the Arizona desert. Back then, of course, my future citizenship made little difference to me. All that mattered was that my parents were Narcisa Arenas and Severo Morales. Their passage from one country to another was also our family's journey from one life to another. Together, my parents faced an unknown future, but one they had taken into their own hands, instead of having it taken from them.

My mother and father were from the state of Guanajuato in central Mexico, an area known as El Bajío. My father came from Silao, which is near the state capital of Guanajuato, fifty-seven miles to the west. My mother was from León, just northwest of Silao. Located in a fertile valley with a magnificent panorama, the town of León was a center for textile and shoe manufacturing. With its many plazas, León was a beautiful sight when approached from the surrounding hills.

It was through my parents' eyes that I was introduced to the spirit of El Bajío, a place of great historical significance spanning hundreds of years. I learned that my mother's father, Don Anastacio Arenas, had witnessed the inundation of the town after the Río Gómez dam broke in 1888, twelve years before her birth. This disaster killed more than two hundred people and left 20,000 homeless. Often, when I complained about hunger or a burning desire for a toy, my mother would respond with fervor; *"Hijo, ¿para qué lloras? ¡Si tu supieras cuánto se perdió en la inundación de*

León!" ("Son, what have you got to cry about? If you only knew how much was lost in the León flood!")

In spite of this tragedy, the town remained progressive and productive. Its population at the turn of the century was actually larger than that of the state's capital. The Bajío region had been an agricultural center even before the Spanish conquest, and it remained so. Because the region was the gateway to the booming mining states of Zacatecas and Michoacán, some of the first Spanish settlements were founded there.

The region's privileged economic position and its correspondingly dense Spanish population contributed to great injustices against the indigenous population. As my grandfather often put it, "Damn those Spaniards." Querétaro and Guanajuato were the two states that made up most of El Bajío, located about 150 miles northwest of Mexico City in the Sierra Madre. My grandfather must have told me a hundred times that a century before my mother and father met, Guanajuato had been the birthplace of Mexico's struggle for independence from Spain.

While my parents were growing up, before the Revolution of 1910, El Bajío was one of the republic's most productive areas. My grandfather often bragged about the abundant corn, wheat and bean fields. All this changed once the Revolution began.

While many books have been written by scholars and journalists about those years, I doubt the human experience has ever been adequately captured. The reality of that era was a harsh one. Young people were conscripted into whatever army was passing through town. Railways, bridges, telegraph lines and roads were destroyed. Money became worthless in people's hands and they couldn't sell what they grew. Fertile fields went unattended. People went hungry. Many died of malnutrition.

For a generation, Mexico's destiny had been in the hands of one man, dictator Porfirio Díaz, who became the bitter enemy of the working class. He encouraged foreign monopolies to expropriate communal lands on a massive scale. He allowed virtual enslavement of thousands of workers, displacement of small farmers and an increase in the number of unskilled laborers on the market. He became so enamored primarily with the French European lifestyle, that it was often said that he publicly renounced his indigenous blood. In certain social strata, he was mocked because he acquired some fine white dust made from rice that he applied to lighten his complexion when he was invited to ceremonies attended by Europeans. His desire for acceptance was that strong.

Díaz's thirty-four year dictatorship was tolerated because it provided economic stability and the beginnings of industrial and cultural modernization. In the end, it brought a decade where the population struggled against widely increasing hunger caused by the quasi-slavery of the people. It unleashed a pent-up revolutionary force that turned the lives of simple people into a great catastrophe that would cost a million lives within a decade, twice the loss of American life in either of the world wars.

My grandfather, Lorenzo Morales, made soap for a living. Silao, located where it was, had many advantages for that trade. It was close to the prosperous haciendas and towns where he sold his product. Lye soap was not easy to produce, at least not the way it was made back then. My teenage father, Don Lorenzo's oldest son, was responsible for getting the product to market and worked as the company's main distributor and dealmaker. He worked the closest with my grandfather, who had three daughters—Juana, Rosa and Manuela—and three sons—Gabriel, Mateo and Severo. My father traveled to the surrounding settlements to sell the soap, using burros to haul it in vats strapped to the animals' backs. My father bragged about how good a tradesman he was and how well he was able to prevent others from cheating him. He often told me, "I developed a talent for selling." He rejoiced in telling everyone, "After all, I started selling tortillas in the marketplace at the age of six."

Those dangerous trips took several days. Bandits occasionally appeared in the countryside. The hunger pangs heightened and thievery became a matter of survival. Simple trust had begun to disappear, and fear was all around. On one of his trips, according to a story which varied with every telling, my father was up in the highlands near San Francisco del Rincón where he camped out with his six burros. Hearing the sound of wolves howling in the night, he thought they might be bandits imitating the wailing noises. As the sounds came closer, he clutched his shotgun and loaded it. Suddenly, he heard a rustling noise approaching the burros. He fired in that direction. The gun barrel exploded with a blast of fire into the darkness. The recoil caused him to roll down the hill. At that moment, he had a sense of what battle in the Revolution was like! Before that, the troop movements of the Revolution had been a distant concern, but with one shot he began to see what fighting on a battlefield was like. He never found out whether he had been startled by bandits or by a coyote.

It was in Don Anastacio's shop that my father first saw Narcisa. She was Don Anastacio's daughter. Her sister Santos was of striking appearance, but Narcisa was exceptionally beautiful. She had long braided hair and green eyes. In remembering his first sight of her, my father always brightened up as he mentioned my mother's gentle, modest femininity. Often, in moments of subdued reminiscence, he would whisper, "*¡Ay qué chula!*" (how beautiful) as he described his memory of her long braids and immaculate home-sewn finery.

Captivated by her subtle charm, he found it difficult to hide his emotions. For the first time in his life, my father became self-conscious in her presence. He also became aware of his pronounced Oaxacan-Tarascan Indian features. He was confident these concerns would not dissuade her heart.

Even at that first encounter, he wanted to tell her about himself. He wanted to know about her. Even though she was very young, he saw the woman inside like a sunburst behind a cloudy dawn. That was the face he hurried to look at the next time he went to Don Anastacio's shop in León: Narcisa's face and her look of hope. It was an impression of her that he was unable to get out of his mind during the months that followed. How he looked forward to his trips to León. Always, upon seeing her, he became nervous and clumsy all over again.

After knowing Narcisa for a year, he was surprised that she accepted his invitation to accompany him on a walk along a hillside not far from León—with her parents' permission, of course. As they strolled on a carpet of colorful wildflowers that had just bloomed after the rainy season, they could see the town and the plazas below them.

Following their walk, the trip back to Silao seemed sad and ponderously slow to my father. His thoughts kept returning to those few precious moments he had spent with her that day. He wondered whether she would think better of him now. Maybe she could come to admire him, even if he hadn't joined up with any army, like her aunts, Ijinia's and Florencia's husbands. Both aunts had gone to live with their sister, Narcisa's mother. My father reflected upon the uncertainty of it all. Was he for Carranza, Zapata, Villa or Madero? Many found it hard to determine whose side anyone was on. No one seemed to be for peace and stability after almost five years of war.

My father had only walked with Narcisa twice, when the army plowed through heavy rains to Tula, San Juan del Río, in the state of Querétaro, just a few miles from Silao. The armies fought a number of battles and had many lesser encounters, defeats and victories. For thirty-eight days, from April 29 until June 5, the opposing armies fought daily over a one-hundred-mile stretch. More than 5,000 men were killed in the dry desert land between Silao and León. My father could not travel and was uncertain what had happened to Narcisa, her family and aunts. Pancho Villa and his men controlled León, and the government's constitutional forces controlled Silao.

My father thought about Narcisa when he saw the wildflowers in the hills and remembered their fragrance. She had captured his heart, but the chances of seeing her again seemed remote in the wake of fractured lives in a country that war had virtually destroyed.

Word finally came that winter, after my father inquired of neighbors who rode the train to León, that Arenas, the shoemaker, and most of his family had survived. After another six months, when my father finally saw my mother-to-be again, he could not help noticing the tears that filled her eyes and the joy they expressed. Although she was by nature shy, she told him how glad she was that he and his family had survived. But the anxiety was far from over. They knew that the next army to come through could bring yet another crisis. It was just a matter of time.

Months later, my father returned to León. Don Lorenzo's soap, produced in Silao, lacked ingredients made scarce by war. Prices rose. In the meantime, Don Anastacio had virtually stopped making shoes, because leather was also in short supply. By then, fortunately, my father had come up with the idea of a northward migration in order to change the family's fortunes.

When my father shared his vision with Narcisa, she was unsure about it. She thought that his idea of going to a faraway country was just as dangerous as staying where they were. Had not the United States just invaded Mexico and patrolled the northern desert in search of Pancho Villa? Although she was sure he wanted to marry her, she feared he might not return from the North. Despite all of these anxieties, my mother finally accepted his proposal and whatever fate might have in store for them. She accompanied him to see the priest at Nuestra Señora de la Luz, who gave them his blessing and married them.

The following week, my father left for California.

North to Moorpark

My father undertook his northward pilgrimage to El Paso and from there to Moorpark, California, on the basis of sheer grit. His fierce determination to offer the family an alternative to poverty and misery gave him the needed strength. He had scarcely enough money for the journey north. He lacked the barest notion of how to prepare himself for the unending, empty distances of the Chihuahuan Desert. Like thousands of immigrants before him, he traveled by rail as far as Aguascalientes and, from there, rode a rattling boxcar to Zacatecas. This was just the beginning of a harrowing trip that my father always described as the worst trial this side of Purgatory. This experience later in life gave him the ammunition to stop us cold when we complained about our modest living conditions. A common refrain was, "You don't know what it is to suffer."

The scant supply of food my grandmother had prepared for him was hardly enough to sustain him on the long road. He kept himself alive by eating small portions and eating only every other day. At one point, he went without food for two whole days. In desperation, during a rest stop along the tracks, he actually stole a sack of food which had been left outside of an outhouse, unguarded. The pirated food got him to El Paso.

My father had suffered severely from the damp and cold in El Bajío, but in the Chihuahuan Desert he faced the debilitating, inescapable heat. The heaviness of fatigue bore down on him, but he was soon to encounter a problem that was even beyond physical hardship. Two devastating armed conflicts had recently rocked North America—World War I and the outbreak of Mexico's Revolution in 1910. The border my father was about to cross had been rife with political tension, even armed hostilities. These thoughts filled his days with increasing dread as he went north. He conversed with fellow passengers about the conditions that existed at the border, where reports of the Americans attacked by Mexican revolutionaries were still fresh in the minds of people. The famous raid by Pancho Villa's men on the town of Columbus, New Mexico, was a frequently recounted and often distorted story. In 1916, a group of armed Villistas had crossed that same border and raided Columbus. There were about one hundred Mexican casualties, while seventeen Americans were reported killed. The raid had been provoked by a switch in the policy of President Woodrow Wilson, which denied Villa access to vital ammunition and small arms previously available to the Villista forces at the border. Villa had felt betrayed. Public, anti-Mexican rhetoric was reaching fever pitch in the United States just as my father was about to enter that country.

By the time my father found himself crossing at Juárez, there had already been much talk about deporting Mexican workers. Less than a month after the Villa raid, the Los Angeles County Supervisors adopted a resolution, requesting federal action in the deportation of what they called the *"Cholos"* whom they considered "very likely" to become public charges. "They are a menace to the health and morals of any community," declared Jim Goodhardt, the head of a noted Los Angeles rescue mission, in a press interview.

This message reached the ears of my father. He was afraid that living in the United States might be living in enemy territory. He wondered if he would be treated as an enemy from a hostile country. How could he build the new life he planned for his family? Could he feel secure in a country which had just seventy years earlier been at war with Mexico? More recently, President Wilson had ordered the U. S. Navy to bombard the port of Veracruz.

Despite these misgivings about an unwelcoming social climate, my father kept alive the dream that he could live in peace among the Americans and obtain a job on the railroad. The more immediate problem he faced was how to get to Moorpark, California. Genaro Bravo, a *paisano* from Guanajuato, had written him of many job opportunities in a place called Moorpark, forty miles north of Los Angeles. The wartime economy had created an intense need for Mexican labor as American manpower was sent to fight in Europe. Despite the anti-Mexican press and the friction at the border, it was common knowledge that unskilled Mexican labor was in demand. This open door would spur on my father and other prospective Mexican immigrants.

As he continued his voyage toward U. S. territory, my father was appalled by the hordes of aimless human beings who had been displaced by the chaos and carnage of the Revolution. Some of the travelers on the train had served under Villa and other famous military leaders. My father listened in awe to the stories about the widespread movement of hungry and demoralized Villistas, their triumphant and failed battles and their horrendous casualties. Eventually, those who were able to travel, wounded or otherwise, struggled back to their ruined villages. Many returned to see the charred wreckage and ravaged fields where their families had once flourished.

Over the years, my father recounted to us the scenes he had witnessed as he traveled north. The once graceful adobe neighborhoods he saw were flattened and the destruction was far worse than what he had seen in Guanajuato. What he saw only heightened his determination to free his family and Narcisa's from such ruin.

Shivering from the cold of the desert dawn, he awoke one day to find the train lumbering its noisy way into the railroad yards on the outskirts of Ciudad Juárez. The Promised Land was finally visible. He paid his two-cent toll and crossed the bridge into El Paso, Texas, the very same day and lost no time undertaking the final phase of his long and exhausting pilgrimage to Moorpark. His insecurity was coming to an end. To buy the ticket to get to California, he had to sell his only personal treasure: three gold coins.

My father took the west-bound train out of El Paso toward Los Angeles. He rode third-class on wooden benches in a smoke-filled car full of animals, shouting and crying children and travel-weary adults. During the first moments of that long ride, my father befriended a fellow Guanajuatense, Juan Echeveste, a man of many more summers than my father's twenty-seven. Echeveste was a well-read man, always carrying an old newspaper under his arm. His dignified manner and colorful mode of dress captivated my father. My father listened, enthralled, as the older man gave his interpretation of the appalling bloodshed during the ten-year revolutionary holocaust. Out of this encounter, a lasting friendship was formed.

When the train reached Imperial Valley, California, the pair got off to seek a few days work in the fields in order to make some much needed money. By chance, they wandered into an orchard laden with a heavy crop of green grapefruit. Although they never found the foreman to seek employment, they gorged themselves on the unripe fruit and immediately paid the awful price—excruciating stomach cramps.

As their misery subsided, so did their fervor for working in Imperial Valley agriculture. They boarded the next train for the coast. In a few short hours, the San Gorgonio Pass and the desert were behind them. Their train coasted through verdant vineyards and orange groves. Within a short time they detrained at the bustling downtown 5th Street railroad depot in Los Angeles.

The travelers soon wound up in the old Placita area. Then, as now, it was the gathering place for our people in Los Angeles. There, they arranged to get a ride on a horse-drawn produce wagon as it headed toward the northern end of the San Fernando Valley. They rode free of charge in return for work as loaders. When their wagon ride ended near the foot of Santa Suzana Pass, they resolved to make the remaining twenty-mile trip on foot. As they walked over the winding wagon trail through the mountains, they were impressed by the lofty, dark red cliffs and gigantic boulders. I have always described the pass as being reminiscent of Pecos, Texas. Walking, to them, was not hard. After all, that's the way they had travelled from one place to another in Guanajuato.

Two days later, they arrived in Moorpark. They were tired, thirsty and terribly hungry. There, they met Don Genaro Bravo, who took them to the Southern Pacific track foreman. They were hired as track hands and immediately celebrated with the first full meal they had enjoyed in weeks. The following day, they reported for their first duties as railroad workers. But the heavy, sledge-hammering drudgery in the blazing heat discouraged them.

Within two weeks, the strain of the railroad job convinced my father that he should definitely look elsewhere for his livelihood. His forté as a worker had been selling and growing crops. "Dirt" (arable top soil), was a sacred base element to him, the sustainer of life. So his next job would be in agriculture, working in the apricot orchards of rancher M. L. Wicks.

What my father did not know was that during the 1860s, large numbers of settlers had come to Simi Valley from as far away as Yucatán. The village of Moorpark, where they had settled then, had a population of only three hundred. But drought and falling cattle prices had forced many of the early owners to sell their land at ruinous prices. Moorpark's fortunes began to increase in 1888 when a railroad was planned to serve the area. By 1901, the tracks were laid to nearby Santa Suzana, and Moorpark was finally linked to the whole economy of California. Almost overnight, the village began to boom.

When my father arrived in Moorpark, he admired the rows of majestic pepper trees along High Street and the Monterey Pines which lined Moorpark Avenue. He was relieved to learn that many *paisanos* from Guanajuato already lived in Moorpark. His friend Manuel Duarte had been an early settler. Duarte had come to help his brother-in-law, Pete Ruiz, with the 1909 bean harvest on a section of land leased from the Freeman Ranch. The following year, Duarte leased twenty acres of peach orchards from the ranch and encouraged Mexican laborers to come to the valley for the harvest.

Albino and Jacinto Corralejo had arrived in Moorpark just before my father did. Albino worked for the Southern Pacific Railroad. Donaciano *"Don Chano"* Rodríguez, who was the barrio humorist, had left Mexico in 1911, just after the Revolution had begun, and arrived in Moorpark to work on the railroad.

My father needed transportation and his employer, Mr. Wicks, eventually agreed to sell him a Model T Ford—an open car, with a fabric top, shiny brass radiator, skinny tires and an Armstrong Starter (a crank handle). It had been in service on the ranch during World War I. It was nearly new. My father planned to use it to convey my mother from Yuma, Arizona, to Moorpark.

My father had listened to Don Juan Echeveste's advice to meet Narcisa at some easily accessible point on the border. It would save Narcisa the confusion of traveling alone in a strange country. The meeting place was to be Yuma on the Sonora-Arizona border. Coincidentally, the plan to meet in Yuma was hand delivered by Mauro Bravo, Genero's brother, who was on his way to *Leon* to bring other members of his family to Moorpark. Juan had asked someone to draw a map for Narcisa with travel instructions. She now had a reasonable understanding of when and where to travel, so she made plans to join her husband and eventually begin a new life in Moorpark.

My father had to promise that he would pay Mr. Wicks for the Model T in installments and would return quickly from Yuma to resume his responsibilities. It was an unusual but important arrangement because, more than anything, it solidified their relationship. To have been trusted by Wicks to leave the state, owing money meant much to my father. Perhaps, in some way, this was how Wicks, a highly moral man, atoned for his part in the pattern of labor abuse that was so prevalent at the time.

My father was so eager to reunite his family that he never gave a thought to Mr. Wicks' motives; he was deeply grateful to his benefactor and impatient to demonstrate his gratitude. So he left for Yuma early one morning.

The Tragedy of Chonita

Back in León, my mother didn't completely understand all that was going on, but she was resolved to join my father in Yuma. She had received his message, some money and instructions. It became clear as the women of our family talked among themselves that they had survived by working together in unquestioned loyalty. To let Narcisa go alone to the North was like sending her into harm's way—they saw it clearly in her bewildered face.

The Arenas family quickly decided that she would not go alone. She would be accompanied on her journey. Her escorts north soon numbered eight women and three children. Rosa Arenas, the matriarch, took charge of Narcisa, as well as of her other daughter, Santos. My mother's aunts, Ijinia and Florencia, who were in their early twenties, had lost their warrior husbands to the Revolution. They had little to stay for and decided that they wanted to leave with the rest of their family. Ijinia took her daughter, Margarita, and Florencia brought her three daughters, Lucita, Cuca and Chonita. Santos was accompanied by her two small daughters, María and Elena.

"This is probably the most frightening trip we will ever make," said Doña Rosa. "So we must stick together." As they bid a final goodbye to the only home they had ever known, they were aware that my mother was pregnant, but she was so small and thin that no one suspected she was already six months along.

Instead of taking the direct northern route, they travelled south to Guanajuato, where they planned to catch a freight train for Guadalajara. Because the cars were filled with troops, horses and ammunition, they rode on top of the train for a while. How she was able to climb the ladder and not miscarry is beyond me. As the frightened women rode, they nearly choked on the smoke from the locomotive and the smoldering ruins of many burning villages.

The women had a limited amount of money and did not want to spend it on food, so they experienced many days of aching hunger. The sun's heat, radiating off the box cars, drained their energy and made my mother dizzy and often tired and sleepy. Only nightfall offered relief as the travelers huddled together to ward off the cold mountain air.

By the second day, the ride atop the cars made the women grow faint from sheer exhaustion. Florencia became nauseous from the daytime heat and the unbearable stench from the horses in the cars below. Chonita, then only ten, clung to her mother and stayed close by her side.

The day's heat increased unbearably in the afternoon. The travelers were squeezed together as the rickety car's lurching rooftop was crowded with others headed for the northern border. Chonita nestled against her mother for security. Florencia glanced down between the cars; then, closing her eyes, she listened to the rhythm of the grinding wheels squealing as they rolled over the noisy, crooked rails. Despite the noise, they all fell asleep. When Florencia woke up, she was comforted by the coolness of the night air. Chonita cuddled up against her on the crowded roof top. Florencia dozed off again, conscious of her daughter's tiny body pressing against her. She resisted opening her eyes, hoping she could forget how faint she was from the penetrating chill of the wind.

Just before dawn, in the cold air thick with smoke, Florencia awoke, barely able to open her burning eyes. In her restless sleep, she had imagined that she felt Chonita sleeping closely by her side. But now, looking down, she felt her heart skip a beat when she noticed Chonita was not there.

Florencia bolted upright and groped for the highest point on the curved roof of the careening boxcar while she struggled against the wind. She looked from one end of the car to the other. Chonita was nowhere to be seen among the sleeping bodies of the other passengers. Her daughter was gone. She felt, at that moment, that she might lose her mind. She fought off the desire to fall back asleep in the hope that she would re-awaken with Chonita safely back at her side. Fearing the unthinkable and unmindful of the peril, she peered over the side of the bouncing car. She could see nothing but rails, ties and darkness.

Florencia had endured many hardships, but nothing could match the shattering thought of her little daughter lying mangled by the tracks in the receding distance and then realizing she had to go on without her. The distraught mother fought the urge to throw herself over the side. Her screams aroused no one. Everyone was obsessed with survival. Her spirit crushed, Florencia wept and shivered through the chill of dawn, hysterically calling out for her lost daughter.

The train slowly continued over the cold rails to Guadalajara. The first threatening leg of the journey was over. The women and children and their possessions were finally allowed inside the cars to continue their journey to the long-awaited rendezvous at Yuma. But little did these brave women imagine what awaited them upon their arrival.

Rendezvous in the Desert

Chonita was gone. The women wept. The train kept on moving as the endless screeching and grinding of steel wheels seared the tragic accident into their minds. The pain of losing Chonita, along with other misfortunes that occurred on this arduous trip to Yuma, lingered for many years. Eventually, the women traveled through the Sonoran Desert to a place just south of the Arizona-California border. They got off at San Luis, a border town on the Colorado River in the Mexican state of Sonora, even though the train's route turned due west toward Mexicali and then on to Tijuana on the California border.

Their journey was far from over. After crossing the border into the United States, they still had many miles of desert to cross. The Sonoran Desert is one of the driest and most desolate pieces of land in the United States. Back then, this trip was difficult even for strong, young men, but Doña Rosa, my aging grandmother, not only made it herself, but saw to the safe passage of her daughters and grandchildren as well. That they made it at all, is a testimony to her indomitable will to survive and her determined leadership.

I can only imagine how courageous they were in facing so many perils on their way into this strange new world. I can visualize their frustration when they did not have enough money for the train trip from San Luis to Yuma. With no money for passage and nothing left to eat, they had no choice but to continue their journey, hungry and on foot. Had they been part of a wagon train, they would have had the advantage of a trailmaster, who knew exactly where he was going. They also would have had their own covered wagon for protection and they would have enjoyed the safety of being with others like themselves. Although weary and exhausted from their interminable trip to the border, the band set out along the railroad tracks, uncertain of what they might encounter ahead. The one thing they were certain of, however, was that they would not get lost if they followed the railroad track to Yuma.

After walking all morning, they finally stopped to rest underneath a railroad water tower near Somerton, Arizona, between the border and Yuma. They were nearing their destination. The dripping water tank, standing on lofty stilts, must have seemed a God-send to them. It provided cool shelter from the brutal sun and fresh water to slake a burning thirst. There, beside that tower, alongside the railroad tracks, the women found orange and banana peels, bread crusts and other scraps that passengers had tossed out of windows when the train had stopped to take on water earlier that day. They devoured the scraps without hesitation. It was a story my grandmother retold often, when we sat down to a typical meal of beans and rice. Never having known the extremes of desperate hunger, it was impossible to imagine what it must have been like for bewildered immigrants, hungrily devouring other people's discards. What helped my mother was her knowledge that she could supplement her diet with *nopales* (cacti), of which there were an abundance in the desert. Her culture had taught her about the life-sustaining powers of desert cacti—the delicious, crimson prickly pears and the pod-like, thick green leaves. I remember she used to prepare them at home—boiled, diced, flavored with garlic and onion and just a touch of cilantro. They were a real treat to us.

As the women continued to walk through the heat, they were told that they would soon reach Yuma. But the trek had been tiring, especially for my mother who could feel the faint kicking of the child within her. Late one afternoon, as they wandered past a cotton field, they encountered a crew of pickers. The contractor gave them an opportunity, reluctantly, to make a few dollars by joining the crew, although they knew nothing about working in cotton fields. The women accepted the contractor's offer under the promise that by the end of the week, they would have enough money to survive until they finally reached Yuma.

The women worked in the cotton fields which were bordered by an irrigation ditch. There, they earned their first American dollars. In later years, my mother often described her bleeding hands when each day's work was done. At the week's end, the harvest came to an end and they pooled their paltry earnings, confident that they had enough to continue their journey. As they prepared to leave the camp, however, fate dealt them another blow. On their final night before preparing to leave, Ijinia, who shared a space with my mother, became very ill, running a high fever.

My mother stayed up all night to take care of Ijinia by herself. In the dark of night, my mother did not know where the rest of the family was. She knew all of the women were extremely tired from their long day in the fields and needed their rest before breaking camp in the morning, so she didn't seek their help. Despite her total fatigue, my mother consoled herself with the idea that her mother and sisters probably would not have been much help, anyway.

In the darkness, just before dawn, my mother finally gave in to sleep. Her pregnancy, days of riding on top of the noisy, lurching boxcar, trekking through the desert, the devastation of losing Chonita and now Ijinia's fever all conspired to exhaust her. She slept through the first light of dawn, through the first signs of movement by the rest of the family and the sounds of others breaking camp. In a state of semi-consciousness, she could faintly hear the voice of the foreman calling out his orders to load the wagons, but she was too drained to pay attention to all of the commotion. In her profoundly exhausted sleep, my mother did not hear when the last wagons that were to have taken them to Yuma pulled out of camp. Their makeshift shelter was behind a giant boulder, close to an irrigation ditch and far from the activity of loading up. When she finally awoke, she was all alone with her feverish aunt. She was also in the advanced stages of her pregnancy.

Doña Rosa had assumed that Ijinia and Narcisa were in the last wagon, so she didn't check on them. She had not seen them among those in the wagons, but was assured by the foreman and the paymaster that they were all present and accounted for. She shouldn't have taken their word. At sunrise, they made their first stop. Then, they discovered that my mother and Ijinia were nowhere to be found in any wagon. Doña Rosa could not stop blaming herself, "How could I have left them behind?" Later, my grandmother was told that another wagon would arrive to load the irrigation pipes and that they would pick up the stragglers and take them to Yuma that following day. But no one ever came for the pipes.

When my mother awoke after the last wagon had already pulled out, she began to run through the deserted campground, searching for the rest of the family. She was horrified when she realized that she and Ijinia had been left behind. They were alone. She cursed the hellish days she had survived and her present abandonment in a strange country with practically nothing to eat. And, she hoped she wouldn't give birth prematurely. As my mother stumbled through the deserted camp, desperately trying to find some-one, she kicked over some rubbish and found a small gunny sack of provisions, including beans, rice and a tin can of lard. She picked it up and went down to the stream, where she drew some water to boil the beans. That, along with the cactus, was their only food, but it was enough to keep them going for a while.

By the second day, my mother, who was young and strong, felt she could hold out for a while longer. But Ijinia's condition was another matter. Although her fever had lifted, she was slow in regaining her strength. My mother stayed close by, fearful to venture too far from her, for both their sakes.

Although it was September, the weather was still miserably hot and the dust made them that much more uncomfortable. Before long, her worst fears were finally coming to pass. In the middle of nowhere, in a country totally unfamiliar to them, there was no food left and no one to help them. They were utterly alone.

My mother worried and prayed. She faced the grim reality that neither Ijinia nor she could survive much longer without sustenance or medical care. And what of her baby? If my mother didn't survive, neither would the child she had carried all those months. If she lost Ijinia to illness, she would have to deliver her baby alone, a prospect that terrified her. The possibility existed that Ijinia's condition would take a turn for the worse, and she couldn't help feeling guilty about that either. If she had not failed to wake up when the travelers decamped, they wouldn't have been in such a predicament.

Early on the morning of the third day, my mother heard the clanging sound of metal coming from a distance across the fields. Although she could not make it out clearly at first, the noise began to sound like cow bells. It was even more difficult to see where the clanging was coming from because of the dust and sand that rolled over the ground like fog, making even the distant mountains barely visible.

Before long, she saw the outline of what appeared to be a country peddler's wagon being pulled by two mules. Ijinia called out. It was an itinerant merchant, one of those who roamed the countryside with a wagon "emporium," like a miniature general store on wheels. The peddler had a little of everything that a person in the fields might need. The sound of heavy iron skillets banging together sounded as sweet as wind-chimes to those who needed those implements in the lonely, migrant worker camps.

My mother was overjoyed to finally see another human being, one who might save them from their sad and potentially disastrous plight. The merchant, however, was disappointed to find that he had arrived at an almost deserted camp, inhabited only by two helpless women in distress.

Despite the merchant's obvious disappointment, my mother believed that his appearance was miraculous. This considerate, bearded peddler could be the salvation of them all: a very ill Ijinia, her unborn first child and, of course, herself. After explaining their dire situation to the old man, he agreed to take them to Yuma and presented them with some jerky to eat. He gave Ijinia his blanket and went out of his way to make them comfortable. He had a kind and warm way about him.

My father, meanwhile, was distressed by my mother's lateness. It had been a week, a long week since he had arrived in Yuma. He had spent most of his days at the Southern Pacific depot, expecting Narcisa to step off one of the incoming trains. He worried that if she was alone or with only one companion, she might have met with foul play. He had heard stories of disappearances in the desert. Over and over, he asked people if they knew the Arenas family or if they had seen a pretty young woman, about eighteen years of age, traveling alone or with another woman.

On the advice of a stranger, my father began to search the migrant camps throughout the area. At last, someone said a family of women from León had worked in the fields and were probably still nearby in a neighboring railroad section camp. Since it was the only one, it was not difficult to find. While my father was frantically looking for my mother, the peddler in the wagon arrived with her and Ijinia and reunited them with their family. It remains a mystery how my mother and Ijinia found my grandmother. I guess that Yuma was just a small frontier village in those days and word traveled fast. The women had not been back together for long when my father finally found them. Relieved to have found his wife, he suddenly awakened to the fact that he had become responsible, not just for his wife Narcisa, but for all the Arenas women who had accompanied her on the journey. For the women, the reunion with my father was not only a relief, it was a reason for celebration.

My father was not interested in celebrating, though. It immediately became apparent that my mother was so close to giving birth that she could travel no further. Only 300 miles away, Moorpark was still too far to reach safely over the rough roads that existed then. It was simply a risk he could not take. Also, it was impossible to take the whole family at one time, even if he had wanted to. The Model T was just too small.

He concluded that he couldn't leave before Narcisa gave birth. His family needed him more than the crops back in Moorpark. Penniless, he was forced to stay in Yuma until I was born.

He now needed to find shelter and food for his wife and her family. He also needed to make arrangements for the birth of his and Narcisa's baby. He was faced with the impending delivery and had nowhere to house my mother. The section yard camp, where he had found them, was certainly not suitable. There was neither privacy nor adequate shelter. All the money the women had earned picking cotton was gone. His money was gone, too, since he had only brought enough for the trip and had not anticipated the delay he was to encounter. They had only one viable alternative, a nearby Indian reservation he had been told about. My father sought out the Yuma tribal elders for help. As it turned out, he trusted the right people. Being welcomed into the world of the Yumas was a relief that renewed his self-confidence.

Yuma

My father met a whole tribe of generous and kindly new friends in this new country. The Quechan people, who lived on the Yuma Reservation, were farmers. In the spring and summer, they would go to their farmland on the river bottom where the Salt River joins the Colorado for the planting and growing season. They lived modestly in large family shelters that were clustered in settlements on the high ground during winter. After the fall harvest, they left their small brush shelters to return to their houses that were built above the flood plains, where the two rivers often overflowed. In their winter homes, earth-covered shelters made from brush and other material, they housed their entire families.

My father's responsibility for his wife and her family seemed not the least bit odd to them. These families pooled their labor, much as Narcisa's had done in the cotton-picker's camp. The Quechan worked together clearing brush, weeding, harvesting and doing other demanding work to ensure the survival of their families.

The Quechans always stood ready to help travelers from other tribes in need of help. My father was of Tarascan and Zapotec Indian heritage. His family came from the Lake Cuitzeo region, situated in a shallow volcanic basin near the northeastern edge of the Tarascan kingdom. The Quechans recognized my father's proud lineage. They gave him materials and taught him the Quechan technique of building shelters. The Quechans showed my father how to build a hut, which they called a "vá na ra." It consisted of willow branches placed along a periphery, which were then bent to form a semi-circular ridge. The framework was then woven in place and covered with clay. So it was in a *"vá na ra"* that I first saw the light of day. On the day of my birth, October 9, 1918, Quechans sympathetic to my parents' plight, placed gift offerings outside of our hut. In keeping with their tradition, they shared with us watermelon, muskmelon, pumpkin, black-eyed peas, and sunflower seeds from their harvest. They also gave us a chicken and cakes made from wildseed meal.

Dionicio was the name I was given at my birth. I can't help but think that my fate, to pursue social justice for people running from revolution and starvation's grasp, was really set in motion in that place. There, two centuries before my birth, a Jesuit priest had presented a staff symbolizing the king's authority and justice to the Quechan tribal leaders. Father Eusebio Kino, the same Jesuit who, in 1697, transcribed the first written records of the Quechan people, had named the place where he encountered thousands of friendly Quechan Indians "San Dionicio," in honor of the saint whose name I bear. As the greatest of coincidences, I was born on San Dionicio's Day of the Catholic calendar.

As I have turned the unique circumstances of my birth over in my mind, I have concluded that these were also somehow the origins of my desire to bring people together to help each other—just as the Yumas had done for my parents and for me. My father's philosophy was molded by this. Thereafter, his advice always took this form: "From my experience with the Quechans, I learned that survival is based on helping each other."

My mother and father were to stay at their temporary shelter among the Quechans for a short time. Eventually, my father found a job at a slaughterhouse and worked there long enough to raise money for the return trip to Moorpark. He killed cattle with a sledgehammer, earning the money to rent a small house near the slaughterhouse. Soon, my mother's family moved in with us.

In just a few days, my father had saved enough money and he prepared us for the trip from Yuma to Moorpark. Unfortunately, the rest of the family would remain behind to plan their own next move. My grandmother, Doña Rosa, hoped that my maternal grandfather, Don Anastasio, and Pedro Ramírez, my aunt Santo's husband, would find them somehow. My mother's father was presumed lost in the Revolution, but Doña Rosa left word in León with neighbors and friends about her destination. She also sent letters to León instructing him to look for them in Yuma.

It was decided that the women would wait in Yuma for their reunion with my grandfather and Uncle Pedro. After those arrangements were made, my father loaded up the Model T and set out on the long journey to Moorpark. My father had converted his shiny 1917 Model T touring car into a pickup by adding a wooden truck bed. The blazing and shifting sands of Yuma's dunes did not discourage him nor the skinny tires and boiling radiator of his Model T. His determination to bring his family to Moorpark conquered every doubt.

Home at Last!

My father's rich brown skin, so helpful to him in establishing a relationship with the Indians in Yuma, now became a liability as he confronted the harsh truths of driving the desert roads of the Imperial Valley. Since his arrival in the United States, he had attributed his unfortunate encounters to the fact that he was single and traveling alone, thereby looking like a threatening stranger to some. But when he stopped to fill a canteen for his family at a roadside store and was refused service, he began to realize that people were behaving malevolently toward him despite the fact that he was traveling with his wife and child. He was puzzled and grew more and more distraught.

Eventually, he found a roadside windmill from which he drew water to quench our thirst. Another time when he needed water for his overheated car, he had to give up a beautiful, hand-woven blanket which had been a gift from the Quechans. He felt as if it had been extorted from him for less than a gallon of water. My father had never paid for water in all his life. He began to wonder what kind of country this was.

In another town, he was refused entrance to a cafe through the front door. We had to enter through the back door and eat on the kitchen steps. A kind black dishwasher patiently made sure that we had a good, complete meal. He thoughtfully gave us some additional food to take with us.

The attitudes he encountered challenged my father's belief that hard work was the great equalizer in the United States. The trip confirmed the worst fears that he had harbored crossing to El Paso. He was beginning to learn that prejudice, because it was apparently the way of life in the United States, might always cast a shadow over his dignity.

While these unexpected experiences demoralized my father, he continued to paint beautiful pictures for my mother of the wonderful new life ahead of them. But in his heart, he feared that dark-skinned, impoverished people were considered a blight on the landscape by many in the United States.

The kindness of that one black man at the desert cafe had a major impact on my father; he developed a tremendous respect for black people. From that day on, he always had a kind word for his black friends, calling them *parna*, a term of endearment that carried special significance to him. It meant "partner."

Later, when he owned his own grocery store, he would frequently send me to the railroad tracks where some black tramps hung out, waiting for a freight train. He would have me bring them back to the store so he could give them a hot meal or bones and scraps for their mulligan stew. I cannot recall him ever making a single disparaging remark about African Americans.

We finally arrived in Los Angeles on a Saturday evening and spent the night there. We camped right in Lincoln Park, now known as the Plaza de la Raza. The hub of the Mexican business and social district, between Sixth and Macy, was crowded with people as we drove past. The next morning, we left Los Angeles at 6:00 a.m. It took us twelve hours to get from there to Moorpark. The dauntless old Model T had made it.

When we arrived, we were hungry. The first item on this tired family's agenda was a hot meal, so my mother fried some eggs. But we didn't have any plates. We had to eat those eggs out of the tin lids of two old lard cans.

In Moorpark, we lived in the adobe house that my father built on Charles Street. Soon after our arrival there, my father returned to his job at M. L. Wicks' ranch, where he eventually became the foreman. As we settled in, my mother began to create a real home for us.

At last, we began to put down roots as a family in a new land!

Model T's and Movies

The end of World War I was close at hand after five bloody years. Just a few days after the U. S. Army wagons pulled out of Moorpark, we received word that the German fleet had surrendered and that a truce had been negotiated. At long last, the guns were silent. It was the eleventh hour of the eleventh day of the eleventh month of 1918. I was one month old.

A year later, my family experienced a different sort of victory: my father was going to Yuma to gather up my mother's family and bring them to their new home. Of course, we didn't celebrate by marching down the street or ringing the church bell or anything as public as that. My father simply made his announcement, got into his new Model T truck and drove off across the desert to get our relatives. By that time, my mother's family had been joined by my grandfather, Don Anastasio, and by Aunt Santo's husband, Uncle Pedro.

That new Model T truck was a victory of sorts for my father—he was very proud of having worked and saved so hard to buy it. The sweet smell of success he felt was matched only by the fragrance of newness that still lingered in the paint and seatcovers when he set out to get the family. But his new and costly transportation was also a reminder to my father of how strictly he had to adhere to the basic rules of survival in order to get ahead.

I've often wondered if his desire to acquire a better life for us and to acquire all those worldly possessions he accumulated over the years also accounted for his notion that there was no room in his life for frivolity of any kind. His demeanor was always dead serious. His all-work-and-no-play attitude was to be an issue of debate between us in later years. It was as though he feared that by letting his guard down, he would be in danger of averting his eyes from the prize.

So the man I came to know as my father was so stern, he hardly ever knew a lighthearted moment. Over the years, he achieved a modest standard of living—he could turn a dollar into ten really fast—and he became increasingly edgy and judgmental. He was not a tolerant man by any means. He led by example and expected his children and other family members to follow his example. That was not always an easy thing to do.

It certainly wasn't easy for Uncle Pedro, who earned my father's disdain during the return trip from Yuma by squandering his money on soft drinks instead of saving it for what my father considered more important things. My father repeatedly warned my uncle that there was barely enough money for food and that he was throwing away what little he had on foolishness, when water would have served him just as well. Time and again, severely outspoken, he reprimanded my uncle for his carelessness with money. Remembering the incident, he would often refer to my uncle as a *viejo tonto*, an old fool, for being so wasteful.

After arriving in Moorpark, my mother's family went to live in an area that later became known as La Colonia, a nearby barrio. There, my grandfather Don Anastasio built his family a typical Mexican adobe house. He set about making a living repairing shoes and soon became known as the *zapatero de Moorpark*, the shoemaker of Moorpark.

Around the time my mother's family settled in La Colonia, the area was stricken with a flu epidemic. It was 1920. Church services and public school classes were suspended and, because there was only one doctor in Moorpark at the time, many people died without any medical attention.

Mrs. Mabel Bradley kept her vigil at the Moorpark telephone switchboard, keeping track of who was sick and relaying messages to doctors in Oxnard, for whom she would describe the patient's symptoms and help him determine which patient should receive his attention first.

During that same year, a man by the name of Ira G. Tanner organized the Moorpark Volunteer Fire Department and was named chief. As a child, I witnessed how the volunteers fought fires—running to use wet gunny sacks, shovels and hoes on the fire at the sound of the alarm bell. They lacked modern pumping equipment. Later on, the fire department acquired two soda acid tanks mounted on a two-wheel cart to fight the brush fires that often erupted on the outskirts of town.

Two years later, in 1922, my father drove off again on a desert trek. This time, he traveled all the way to El Paso to get members of the family who had arrived at Juárez by train. Almost our entire family had relocated to the U.S. My world was becoming complete with the arrival of my grandfather Don Lorenzo and grandmother Doña Hilaria, who brought with them my aunts and uncle: Juana, Rosa, Manuela and Gabriel. My uncle Mateo had arrived ahead of the others and had accompanied my father to El Paso. My family was part of the increasing number of Mexican families coming to the area, which was growing rapidly—one extended family at a time.

Among those families were Luis and Teresa Borja, who arrived in Old Simi from Romita, Guanajuato in 1924. Susano and Guadalupe López, accompanied by their grandson, came to visit friends in the Simi Valley and decided to stay. Each new family that came brought new stories about the Revolution and their experiences in its tragic aftermath.

Moorpark was booming, at least by our small town standards. The year after my grandparents arrived, a rancher,

Charles Holland, gave my grandfather permission to build the first adobe house on his ranch; and others wanted to do the same. That inspired Holland to seek a bank loan in 1923 to subdivide his land into lots. That section in Moorpark later became known as Colonia Virginia. There were those who speculated that the colony was named after Holland's wife. Others said it was named after a woman evangelist who did missionary and social work among Mexican families. Located on the east side of town, Colonia Virginia rapidly became home for many of the families who worked on the local ranches.

Modern technology was also becoming part of Moorpark as the number of telephones steadily increased and both electricity and natural gas were installed in most of the homes and commercial establishments. Electricity in the area came about as a result of the first electric generator being installed in 1919 at the Wolff Ranch at Spring Street and Los Angeles Avenue after the Southern California Edison Company purchased the Pacific Light and Power Corporation.

But all this progress eluded our people. Long after the Edison Company had built its Moorpark subdivision in 1922 and electricity had become increasingly available throughout the valley, we still lived in a home illuminated by flickering, smelly kerosene lamps. Other townspeople, including the Wicks, the Stratherns and other large ranching families, were much more fortunate. They were given free electricity in exchange for the right-of-way through their properties. Those privileges, due to our different social standing, were not unusual.

Even as a child, I began to understand why my father worked such long hours and why he saved every penny that he could. His foresight, as foolhardy as it may have seemed to many of his contemporaries, could not be ignored.

Despite the fact that we were Mexicans, we were one of the few families that owned a new Model T Ford. And, my father never doubted for a moment that he could fulfill our dreams for a home of our own one day. In a way, I feel I inherited his sense of determination and dogged persistence.

As a child growing up, I witnessed the passage of Moorpark from a hearty frontier to a rural area to one quickly being encroached upon by exploding urbanization.

In the early 1920s, a hit-and-run driver struck and killed M. L. Wicks as he stepped into a Los Angeles street. From that moment on, everything for my family began to change.

Early in his life, the frugal Mr. Wicks had written his prescription for a long life. His journal was found after he died, buried in a desk drawer among other personal possessions. He called it "How to Live 100 Years." His formula for a long life consisted of chewing every bite of food until it became a "creamy consistency," drinking two quarts of "aerated, distilled water," resting, exercising, avoiding meat, narcotics and stimulants, keeping a positive attitude, shunning coddling, doing good, giving quick, cheerful, practical assistance, recognizing that God's Kingdom was within you and striving to show it to your neighbor. I don't know how my grandfather got a copy, but when Mr. Echeveste translated it, I was all ears.

After his death, Mr. Wicks' son, Percy, who had served as an army major during World War I, returned to the area to manage his father's affairs. Percy Wicks, in contrast to his father, liked to think of himself as a celebrity. Since his house was on the edge of the barrio, we would often see him in his sporty knickerbockers, driving around in a big, fancy automobile and living alone in an imposing, but quaint house.

My family was still living in the modest, three-room adobe house, which had been our home for seven years.

After the birth of my sister Socorro and my brother Trinidad, our house on Charles Street became too cramped for our family, so my father decided it was time to buy another piece of property on which he would build a bigger home. In 1925, two years after I started school, my father got an opportunity to buy a piece of property in Walnut Canyon from good old Percy Wicks. The lot, which was just a mile away from Main Street, was to become another of my father's hard earned victories. The lot was also big enough for my grandparents, Don Lorenzo and Doña Hilaria, to build a house right next to ours.

Because my father couldn't build the house until he paid off the note, he decided we could live temporarily in a tent on the property. So, he moved us out of the adobe house and into a tent until he could afford to buy the materials he needed to build our new home. Our grandparents moved into another tent on the empty lot with us. Outside our tent, which was located halfway up a hill along a dirt road, my father also constructed a corrugated tin kitchen, which was shared by both families.

Making a small down payment on property in those days was a big obligation and a risky proposition, but my father saw it as an opportunity to move up in the world, so he took it. It mattered little to him that by living in a tent we would have to give up some of the conveniences we had already become accustomed to. Credit was scarce in those days, and what little he could spare from his meager wages was applied toward paying off the property loan.

There were, however, some advantages to the new property my father had purchased. Situated where it was, the panoramic view of the hills and valleys from our lot was just as awesome, if not more beautiful, than that of Wicks' home, which was located at the summit.

Even though our living conditions had changed slightly, our family life went on as usual. During the time we lived in the tent, my mother gave birth to three more children—Antonia, Elvira and Timoteo.

By the age of six, I had already been taught to accept the responsibilities of the eldest child. I would often work ten hours at Percy Wicks' ranch during the summer. It was a chore most children performed at my age, and by the time they were twelve, were usually graduated to picking fruit. Later on, when we needed less supervision, we were shown how to dry the fruit. On top of that, every morning I had wood to chop for my mother.

Apricots were shaken from the trees, picked by hand and put into fifty-two pound boxes before being hauled off to a shed, where workers like myself, cut the fruit in half and placed it on trays after removing the pits. The trays were then placed on cars and rolled into a smudge house on narrow steel rails, where they were smoked with sulfur fumes for about twenty-four hours. Afterward, the fruit was placed out in the sun for several days to dry. That completed, the trays were then stacked up and the dried apricots were scraped off. When this was completed, the empty trays were filled again with new apricots and the process began all over again. The pits, which were never discarded, were also dried, then sacked and sold. I would come home late in the evening, exhausted, with my hands blistered and a burning sting under my fingernails from the mud and acids of the apricot juice.

In the 1920s, the sleepy depot, built in the so-called "steamboat gothic" motif, gave the town some of its distinction and even became the town's landmark and symbol. It was a popular place that often appeared in movies filmed in town. Just beyond where Don Anastacio and Doña Rosa lived, the Santa Susana Pass appeared on the screen as the dry gulches and rocky canyons of many cowboy movies. The landscape looked like the quintessential wild west that movie makers demanded.

The legendary filmmaker, Jack Warner, once appeared at our grammar school to recruit children for the mostly cowboy movies on location in our area. Many of us played the roles of "Indians." Working as a movie extra provided us a way to get excused from school and make, as I remember it, $2 per day. They also fed us a box lunch. There were movies made with Hoot Gibson, Buck Jones and Ken Maynard. The last Tom Mix film made in our area was filmed at the Strathern Ranch. One Gary Cooper movie was made near Moorpark. In it, he raced across the tracks and just barely made it while the huge locomotive came barreling down on him. But in the actual filming, as I witnessed it, the action took place very slowly, so there was never any danger of a crash. The film was later sped up to make it look like he made it just in the nick of time.

My buddy Chon Corralejo and I would show up on my sulky, a horse-drawn cart, at the movie locations, even when I wasn't hired to see if there was anything left over from the lunch boxes. I must have become a fixture, riding out there looking for work as an extra in a sweat-stained, brown fedora hat. That was my signature look. Their personnel would often give me the leftover lunches. These were real treats—fried chicken and biscuits or roast beef sandwiches—that I took home. My family had so little money that appearing in a movie, getting excused from school, making a few bucks and getting the box lunches was like a holiday celebration. I appeared in perhaps ten movies and visited the locations of many more. If a cowboy movie was shot in or around Moorpark with Indian children in it or with a Mexican setting, one of the children was probably me.

During lean times, the Strathern Ranch was often con-
tracted out as a movie location, which later became a
favorite spot for filmmakers because of its grazing animals,
a train that passed through the range and its rugged mountain background. As a movie location, the ranch became
best known for a sheep-grazing scene in "The Life of Louis
Pasteur," starring Paul Muni. Much later, scenes from the
television series "Gunsmoke" were shot at that ranch. Other
ranches became prominent backgrounds for the movie-making industry. For instance, the last scene in "Through Train
to Arkansas," starring Bob Burns, was filmed at the nearby
Birkenshaw Ranch.

Watching all this movie-making was exciting for me as a
child, although it was just another facet of our life that we
all took for granted. This was a time of transition in the film
industry, when the silent era was ending and "talkies" were
beginning to flourish. Although I didn't realize it at the
time, the movie industry was experiencing a Golden Era
that would forever change the City of the Angels, making it
the film capital of the world. Tinseltown!

As a child, the art of movie-making never failed to
amaze me. Once, I remember a movie crew setting up long
overhead poles along Main Street. They had wires at the
end, like fishing poles. The wires were attached to a contin-
gent of the Keystone Cops—the mustachioed, harum-scarum
uniformed comics who took their name from the production
company that featured them. When the director called for
action, these slapstick, silent film actors came careening
down the street behind a car they were chasing, then suddenly collided with another car. Bodies flew out in every
direction, yanked by the poles and wires that were attached
to each of the actors.

It was fascinating for me to see how comedy was created
by exaggerated behavior and the element of surprise, espe-

cially at my age. I was mainly captivated by the idea that some kind of forethought had gone into producing these kinds of scenes in order to create comedy, and how even an accident could be made to appear comical. I was aware that someone had to think through every aspect of such a scene and pull the strings.

Even more exciting was the arrival on the set of a big star, such as humorist Will Rogers, Sr. It didn't take a genius to figure out why he was so popular, especially when he was known for handing out silver dollars, a lot of money in those days. One of the most difficult decisions I ever had to make as a kid, when he gave me one of the silver dollars, was whether I should spend it or keep it as a souvenir. I could hardly wait to spend it.

One of my more earthy recollections of Will Rogers, however, is the special day when he had to pause from filming to use our "bathroom." Bathroom was how it was referred to in school, but in reality we just had a stinking outhouse. I was so excited when I realized that he had gone into our outdoor "facility." I was so thrilled about it that I promptly ran out and hung a colorful sign on the toilet door that read, "Will Rogers Took a Piss Here."

My father owned three Model T Fords in the 30s and 40s. He kept and drove one until the day he died. On one comical occasion, while driving one of these venerable cars, he got mixed up with a parade of Model T's being filmed for a movie called "King's Row." In the confusion, he bumped into none other than actor Ronald Reagan, who happened to be filming that day along with stunning actress, Ann Sheridan, who made an unforgettable stir when she visited my father's store to buy a Coke.

My father could never have envisioned his son and daughter-in-law having dinner in the White House State Dining Room with the same Ronald Reagan. How proud he

would have been to know a descendant of his Tarascan forefathers was invited to dine with the President. From Walnut
Canyon to the White House!

On another occasion, my father bought a plow horse
from Joel McCrea and his actress wife Frances Dee, who had
purchased a 2300 acre spread about five miles from our
store. I went along as a translator and I invited him and his
wife to my home for a birthday fiesta. He couldn't make it,
but he sent my sister a bag of wonderful Hollywood sou-
venirs and an autographed photo.

Once, I played the part of an elephant-boy for a week. It
was both horrifying and exciting to lead the huge pachy-
derm through his paces in a local make-shift jungle at
Thousand Oaks, just seven miles from Moorpark. The movie
was produced by Duncan Reynaldo, who became famous in
the movie, "Trader Horn."

While I watched the movie-making all around me, my
father continued accepting contracts from Adolph and
Charlie Gisler to work at their ranches. By 1924 their walnut trees were producing exceptionally well, which meant
my father was kept busy contracting Mexican families from
Moorpark, Santa Paula and Los Angeles as work crews. The
crews stayed in bunk houses and tents on the ranches
where they worked as tree shakers, pickers, hullers and dry-
ers. My family also camped out on the ranches with the
other families, and I would help pick walnuts from five to
seven thirty in the morning, before going to school.

I'm Not Different, Am I?

About the time I started school, a Miss Edna Jaqua was hired exclusively to teach the Mexican school children. She was assigned to grades one through four. In these first four grades we were separated from the Anglo children. Our classes were held in a separate building that had a dirt floor and a leaky roof. We weren't privileged enough even to have flushing toilets. No one bothered to clean up the mess in the outhouses that twenty-plus children used. School officials segregated us racially by stating that we did not speak English well enough to be with the Anglo students.

Though we were separated in this manner from the Anglo children in these lower grades, in neighboring Simi, Mexican children were segregated up to the seventh grade. But by the fourth grade, the lessons of inequality were instilled in us. Our parents hardly gave any thought to the traumatic effects on their children. Still, all of us pledged allegiance every morning. We hardly knew what the words meant. We never gave any thought to the idea that we were anything other than American citizens.

In a way, I was more fortunate than those I was growing up with because I had a father who must have instinctively known that we were starting from behind and, for that reason, he insisted that our schooling come before all else. Time and again, he lectured us about our future, insisting that it did not lie in the fields. I remember that my father had plans for me. He didn't want me to end up working as a farm laborer. When I reached twelve years of age, he pulled me out of the fields and forbade me to return. Not having known any other kind of life, I wondered if this new privilege he had given me was merely an act of defiance on his part.

After all, he had taken away from our household an important source of income, as meager as it was. And, my wages would have enabled me to be an equal in the eyes of my friends, whose fathers insisted they go to work in the fields.

At that time, it was customary for entire Mexican families to go out into the orchards to begin the day's work at sunup. To have a child who was able-bodied and old enough to earn his keep merely stay home and go to school was rare. The Anglo society around us believed in the mystical qualities of the work ethic and spent a lot of time praising it; we, on the other hand, spent most of our time practicing it. Far more people believed in the idea of work than in the exercise of work, as we knew it. The evidence was in our hands, which were stained the color of mahogany from picking walnuts. We came to know exhaustion better than most people. It was something to which we had become accustomed by the early age of six, simply for survival.

As a child trudging to school after leaving the Adolph Gisler Ranch orchards, I remember my clothes were often soiled and wet with perspiration. The dust that swept up from the ground as I walked to school left a grimy film all over my clothes and body. Then, after school, I would hurry back to the ranch and return to the orchards to pick up where I had left off in the morning.

Although our teachers knew that most of us worked in the orchards before going to school, they were nevertheless insensitive about our soiled clothing and faces. I recall one particular instance when, after working in the walnut orchard and then walking to school over the dusty road, I became the subject of a nurse's displeasure because of my unkempt appearance. It was vaccination day and all the children were lined up to receive their shots. When the nurse looked at me, she greeted me with a frightening scowl. She was pop-eyed, double-chinned and hostile. Since my arm was covered with dirt, the cotton soaked with alcohol naturally turned black when she rubbed my arm with it. "When was the last time you took a bath?" she asked in a loud voice. The other children standing in line giggled as they watched. Some of the Anglo girls covered their mouths to hold back their laughter. Innocently, I responded, "Saturday." Everyone in class laughed, unable to contain themselves any longer. What did I know? The nurse had asked me a question and I responded as truthfully as I could. The mocking laughter of my classmates haunted me. I was already in the fourth grade, but until that moment, I had truly been blind to the strongly felt differences between us. I had thought of them as my friends. I realized then the infinite distance that existed between them and me. I sensed such downright meanness as I stood there, speechless, watching their mockery. I was simply a kid from the orchards who lived in a tent. The Anglo kids came from clean homes that had flushing toilets. They took a bath on Saturday nights in smooth porcelain tubs, while we had to take turns bathing in an old iron wash tub in water that had been heated over a wood fire in the back yard.

And to make matters worse, the nurse had singled me out to the class as an example of a person with bad hygiene, and she lectured them on why it was important to wash, as I had failed to do. "This boy smells bad," she told them. Then she handed me a note to take home to my mother, adding that I needed to go home immediately and take a bath.

Wanting desperately to run away or get out of that room, I reached for the paper so I could leave, but she held onto it so tightly, I couldn't take it from her. Pulling back, she added to my disgrace by declaring that she was going to check me over for "cooties." That's what they called lice back then. Finally, she sent me on my way with instructions that I go home and bathe and ask my mother to wash my head with kerosene.

That horrifying experience only led to future disappointments. By her insensitive outburst, that nurse gave my classmates a social lesson at my expense. In her own way, she was instructing them to avoid me and others like me, no matter how much we might have wanted to fit in. Their mocking laughter was like a signature on the social contract that says, "If you're white, you're alright." Even dirty Anglo kids with "cooties" were usually handled with more discretion than we were.

My head must have hung very low with embarrassment that day. I felt like a miserable outcast. The world was divided between the clean and the dirty. The clean children were the non-Mexicans. I was only seven years old, but as I walked home that day, I knew, instinctively, that even though I was an American by birth, I was beginning to feel that my life was never going to be easy. There were silent rules about being an American that had nothing to do with being born in this country.

My predicament was only compounded at home. After I explained to my mother what had happened, she told my father. He gave me the thrashing of my life for having shamed the family in that way. He didn't give me a chance to explain. For my father, teachers represented the highest authority. He wouldn't allow anything to stand in the way of my obeying them. He absolutely refused to accept any excuse for my having missed school, even when it was my school that had sent me home.

As a result of this and other humiliations, I began to withdraw. I began to walk alone. I went to school, was a good student, obeyed my teachers, but all the while, I felt isolated from the teachers and my classmates. For me, school was a form of exile imposed upon me by a stern father who repeatedly warned me to stay away from the other kids and forbade me to run around with them. I had never been an outgoing child to begin with, but now I had even more difficulty in expressing myself. So I said little. In fact, I became such a quiet child that most of the kids in Walnut Canyon and around Moorpark dubbed me "The quiet canyon kid," a nickname that was to stay with me for a very long time.

Despite the segregation and prejudice I confronted, a little star began to glimmer on my horizon when I was eight years old. The star was Mrs. Mary Henry, who taught our second grade. She seemed to like me. Perhaps it was because I was such a quiet, obedient pupil. She won my heart for keeps when she let it be known that she frowned on the practice of washing my mouth out with soap and water—something I had experienced in the first grade.

Mrs. Henry remembered me long after I finished her class. She gave me employment at her bantam chicken farm. I cleaned the chicken pens and she paid me a quarter or so, and she would give me a glass of milk for good measure.

While I gulped down the fresh milk, she talked to me about what to do about the things that interested me. "Go to the library," she said. "Go to the library." At that stage of my life, that seemed premature advice. After all, the only things I was learning to read were "Chicken Little" and "Mother Goose."

But later in my grammar school years, I did go. That's where I began to explore the world inside my mind and found a place somewhere between real events, dreams and aspirations. I found that place in biographies. From reading my favorites about George Washington Carver, Simón Bolívar, Napoleon and Benito Juárez, I started forming the idea that things could be made to come out according to one's wishes.

When I was seven, I found that when you're serious, people take an interest in you. That wasn't the case for Güicho Ortega or Ray Corralejo and some of the other kids in the neighborhood. They were rough, tough and brutal. They found strength in numbers and seemed committed to their school pranks. In my case, I had to walk that fine line between getting identified as a complete loner and becoming beholden to the gangs. I found it almost impossible to utter vulgarities. My grandfather's and father's discipline had rubbed off on me.

Later, in the seventh grade, I used to talk to Mr. Robert Carmichael, my school's principal. He took a liking to me because I was studious, even though he was openly a very prejudiced man. "You're the only Mexican kid that I know around this place who looks intelligent," he would say to me.

About the attitude of teachers, however, we pupils were often confused about the reason for their hostility to us. What, exactly, was it we did wrong? It seems we were punished for just trying to learn.

Other things happened, too. I was in grammar school the entire time we lived in a tent. One day, my teacher had us describe our homes. Evelyn Everett, a wealthy rancher's daughter, went into a lot of detail about where the parlor, drawing room, dining room, bedrooms and other parts of her expensive house were. Her father owned the largest apricot orchard in our valley. When my turn came, I didn't say anything. I was immobilized. Most of the Anglo kids almost died laughing. They all knew I lived in a tent. While living there was fun and an adventure to my brothers and sisters, none of the Anglo kids saw it that way. I did say, however, that my mother had a beautiful garden, bordered with rows of stones which were painted white.

Another time, we were asked what our fathers did for a living. "My father has a ranch" or "My father has a hardware store" were some of the answers. Then my turn came. "Well, Dionicio?"

I was already notorious as the quietest kid in our neighborhood. Now I felt desperation and ridicule. You see, my father's job was cleaning the manure out of the Wicks' barn during the winter and spreading it in the orchard.

Then came another unforgettable tragedy. One summer day, when I was fifteen, I drove my father's Model-T pick-up, without his permission, to the Sinaloa Ranch in Simi Valley, which was owned by Bill Robertson, a well-known grower. My buddies Pancho Almaguer and Roberto Arroyo, came along. It was about five miles from where we lived. We took sandwiches for lunch to eat at the artificial lake on the Robertson property. The lake was used for irrigating the lemon and orange groves. A small, badly-constructed home-made raft had been left on the shore and, although it was too small to hold us, the three of us climbed onto it and drifted out to the center of the lake and into an area covered by treacherous floating moss.

We were too heavy for the raft. That, along with water-logging, pulled the raft down. We started sinking. I didn't know how to swim, but somehow I paddled back up and held on to the capsized raft that had floated to the surface. But Roberto, even though he could swim, never made it back up. He got entangled in the thick moss under the surface. The bread from our sandwiches floated there on the water where I expected his head to bob up at any moment. Roberto never came up.

When the authorities delivered me to my father, I received one of the worst horse whippings in my life. I thought he was going to kill me. As a result, I have never learned how to swim and do not want to. I still have a phobia about going into water.

Crash

From my point of view, living in Walnut Canyon, the largest of three Mexican barrios, had four important advantages. The first advantage was that my barrio was only a half mile from Main Street. The hill behind our row of houses along the inclined road was a perfect escape route and short cut. My dog, Barbón, and I roamed far and wide whenever the mood struck us. Another advantage was Walnut Canyon's slope. But most important of all, however, was that it provided solitude.

When the rough road leading up the hill was finally smoothed over with pavement, it became a half-mile long esplanade and just perfect for our games. The new road was like the Indianapolis Speedway to Chepe Durán, Pancho Almaguer and my brother Trinidad, who helped me build something that resembled a soapbox scooter. We had racing in mind, although not one of us had ever done it before. We thought about what a thrill it would be coming down the slope at break-neck speed. Only there was one small detail we neglected to think about when building the racer: How to stop it when it reached the bottom of the hill.

That, notwithstanding, the coaster fairly flew on its generously greased iron rims. On the first dry run, we passed an astonished farmer with a wagonload of hay on the way down. The thrill ended abruptly in front of the high school, since we had to crash in order to stop. Unfortunately, we rolled over several times before ending up in a ditch.

As we lay there trying to figure out what had happened, I realized that something was wrong with my hand. While we sat there, not knowing whether my hand was broken, or, what to do about it, we heard a tremendous, earth-shaking thud. Moments later, we saw a burst of light followed by a tremendous explosion on top of the hill, followed by a huge column of smoke rising in the air. At this point, it didn't matter whether my hand was broken or not. The realization that a plane had crashed wiped out any thoughts about ourselves. We ran up the hill to where we had started our ride. The farmer we passed on our way down was there, helping the pilot move away from the flaming aircraft. The plane was a total wreck, burning out of control. In a way, it was as if we, who were going down were crashing, and those who were going up were crashing, too. That's what it was like just before the Depression.

My Future Illuminated

We were always busy at home. My father and mother planted a large garden in a plot of land in the back yard. They put me to work growing cauliflower, tomatoes, coriander and other vegetables and herbs. There were some walnut trees on the property left over from the orchard that had previously occupied the space. My chores included irrigating the plot and feeding the pigs, chickens, and rabbits. One time, my brother Trini and I forgot to feed the goats. They have to be fed every day, especially during the time they are giving milk. It was a real bother because we had to gather stalks and other remains in the fields after the black-eyed peas were harvested. That's what we fed the goats. But we forgot this one day.

My father came home at midnight and realized what had happened. He got us up in the middle of the night. Out in the dark field, we filled the gunny sacks with dried feed. Coyotes started howling. The barks and howls came over us like a sudden, bone-chilling wind. The experience taught us three big lessons—be prompt in getting chores done, others counted on us and there is a consequence when you don't. We learned that if you don't do as you should, the coyotes will haunt you with their eerie howls in the middle of the night.

In addition to the wonderful natural surroundings of Walnut Canyon, we had other places of diversion as children. The chassis of my father's first Model T sat in our backyard. The junk car was hollowed out and boarded up so that all that remained of the converted truck was its shell. I painted it bright yellow and white with the only paint around and planted a white carnation garden around it. My mother called them *claveles blancos*, and they were her favorite flower.

My neighborhood pals and I loved to play inside, making something of a clubhouse out of it. In later years, I converted it into a little studio and practiced my mandolin there after our next door neighbor, Don Timoteo Flores, taught me how to play. I also spent my time there reading and drawing. But mostly, I used it as a getaway, a place to be alone with my thoughts.

The books that I stole or borrowed accumulated inside the Model T studio. This is where my life-long love of reading began.

My mother would find me reading a lot. *"¿Qué es lo que quieres hacer en la vida?"* (What do you want to do when you grow up?) she would ask when she saw me daydreaming. "I want to be famous," I answered naively.

"What's that?" she wanted to know. "How is it that you want to be famous?" I could not explain to her what I meant—I wasn't even sure myself. I knew I wanted to do something of consequence, something that mattered, something significant. Finding that leverage point took a long time. But early on, I tried explaining to my mother how the family experience, combined with the biographies that I checked out of the library, were working on me. Those were the wrong words for the right concept.

I had many conversations like that with my mother. She drew me out, listened to me patiently and tried to understand what I was trying to say. Sometimes, she would talk to me inside the tent while she sat knitting. She even tried to help me with my homework, regardless of her not understanding it. What matters is that she tried.

I suppose I was no different than any other product of early childhood. It was my mother that I talked to more than anyone else at that time. My mother was always there when I needed advice, when I was crying or when I was hungry. I was hungry often. Since we had no money for tea or coffee, she would pull leaves from our lemon and walnut trees for that purpose. How happy she made me feel when I was consumed with pangs of hunger and there she was, waiting for me with a cup of hot tea. That, coupled with the aroma of freshly made tortillas greeted me when I got home from school. That combination of pungent and sweet scents remains with me today. She could take anything, like squash blossoms she picked from the garden, and make *quesadillas* with the addition of other ingredients she could find. A vanilla malt never tasted as sweet as those things she made out of nothing. Every Mexican American family's elders I know, relive these glorious memories of home.

I agreed with my father that she was breathtaking. A small woman, no more than 100 pounds. Her outer beauty was reinforced by her sweet character.

She was a devout Guadalupan Catholic, having faith sometimes even in deep-rooted, pious superstitions. Her spirit lived with many saints, especially *La Virgen de Guadalupe*, whose image she tacked not only over her bed, but over the kitchen door, as well. She was surrounded by spiritual forces all the time. She lived with naïveté because of the smallness of her world, confident that being spiritual would cure the sickness of both the soul and the body.

As petite as she was, she was able to survive all the tragedies that she was forced to endure. These continual hardships would have crushed a lesser person.

When we grew up in the Depression, every family had to do without. We were no different. We still had to chop wood, heat the water over a wood fire, cook on a wood stove and bathe in a galvanized iron tub. She never complained nor was she ever confused about her duty to her family. She was my mother, a real Christian, from a real

Christian household in the days when survival was the main concern.

My mother knew how to do everything: milk the goats, skin a rabbit, build her own chicken coop. Yet, she found time at the end of the day to fix herself up to receive my father when he came home.

My father, on the other hand, was always busy making a living and paying off the property. My grandfather started to become a greater influence on me than my father in those early years. Later, my father was to play more of a role in my life. But when I was very young, he was isolated from much that was going on in the household. When he wasn't at work, he had too many other things to do around the tent, such as mending the fence, turning the land over for our garden or feeding the goats. He would get up at four in the morning and start hammering or shoveling. Seldom would he have a conversation with my mother or with us, he was so busy attempting to bring the comforts of home to the tent.

My father was a combination of two major personality traits. So much so, that he could have been playing the part of two people. In character, he was double-fisted, bombastic, assertive; this was when he was at work. But at home, surrounded by his family, he lived by a dominant word which permeated all of our lives together, the word *"respeto"* (respect). Mild-mannered and gentle at home, he would never fail to send a contribution in case of a neighbor's death. Around the house, he spoke in modulated and kindly tones. We never heard him speak in a profane manner. The value he placed on respect was first and foremost. No one in his family would smoke or drink beer or hard liquor within the confines of his home.

One of his dominant quarrels was based on his concept of *"machismo."* He most certainly did not agree with the typical Anglo conception of the meaning of the word, which involved disregard and disrespect toward women. A *macho*, he would say, was a horse. A *macho* is what pulled his plow. He worked like a horse, because of his responsibilities. *Machismo*, to my father, meant that one met his responsibilities to his family, at whatever effort and sacrifice. He felt that the fulfillment of family responsibility was the highest human obligation. He literally killed himself, working as a *"macho"* man, as much as 20 hours per day, in order to see his family provided with the very best that he could make available. He sacrificed to get us out of Walnut Canyon, out of the leaky, floorless tent, into a spacious house on High Street, Moorpark's main residential street. He demanded of himself that he be in a position to reinforce the financing of my higher education.

With such seriousness of life purpose, he could not have imagined that some men would, one day, shave their heads, or leave their hair shoulder length, or strike a woman, or wear earrings, or engage in loud talk or have ill manners.

My father believed that a *"macho,"* in a blue shirt or a white shirt, should be able to conjure up the moral fiber to confront any life situation... even the boss, in defense of his rights, as an employee. A *"macho,"* who met his definition of that status in life, would certainly stand up and be counted for what was right. To my father, a man who beat his wife was a *"rata"* (a rat).

My father, with minimal formal schooling, learned basic accounting and bookkeeping from my grandfather. I suppose my father had a basic philosophy of life which later would stand me in good stead in the career I chose.

In a way, what appeared to be an antiquated traditionalist example, was actually a manifestation of how my ancestors, from way back, had passed on their culture by word of mouth, always with the hope of better things for the family.

Cleanliness, neatness and grooming were the basics of my father's expression of pride. To him, being dirty or slovenly, even without a bath, was no excuse whatever in poverty. Saturday night and Sunday, he was the picture of a dapper gentleman, brimming with self confidence, ten-gallon hat and all.

During the late 1920s, we would sit around after dinner for my father's and grandfather's storytelling time. All of our neighbors would come to our house to hear my grandfather tell stories. To me, he was one of the greatest storytellers in the world. My father wasn't bad, either. They would sit around a campfire that provided light in the dark and gave warmth in the chill of the night. The tales they told were about what they saw, what they heard, what they believed and about coming to the United States. There were also horror stories about the witches who bled people at night or came in through the window, or took out people's eyes. All that was quite frightening to me.

The neighbors would sit around, sometimes awed, sometimes amused, and often came back for more. Don Lorenzo would stand up to tell his stories. He was tall and thin, like a classic Tarascan gentleman. He would have made a good minister because he had the body language of one and a captivating demeanor. His intonation was strong and his descriptive words made his virtual orations sound like sermons. When Mexican politics was his subject, he would stand on the hard dirt and preach his critical beliefs by the fire that burned late into the night. His robust features made his words hit their mark, enhancing the morals he drew from. He had strong opinions and kept up with current events, but was also unusually sensitive. With a passion, he would frequently say, *"Yo tengo que irme a mi tierra*" (I must return to my own country). "*¿A qué va, abuelito?*" (What will you do there, Father?) I wanted to know. "Smell the fragrance of the flowers in Guanajuato, which I have never found here in the United States," he said. "For that. The fragrance of the flowers in the hills!" I think that was his metaphor for his homesickness for Guanajuato, the mystery behind the underlying feeling that he was less than complete and why this place made him feel that way. "I want to be buried underneath those flowers."

My grandfather often looked tired and weatherworn. In the midst of struggling to survive, he had been an itinerant school teacher who had taught basic literacy in remote locations. He was likely unprepared for the hard life that rained down upon us. He had been the genius behind starting the soap factory in Silao and dealing with production and distribution. Now he was relegated to long hours of work in the fields and orchards.

Don Lorenzo would get up early in the morning to buy *El Heraldo de Mexico* from a passing newsboy and he would read it. Then he would make me sit in front of a mirror and read it. "*Léalo,*" (Read it!) he'd say, "because you're losing your ability to speak Spanish." I would have to read the Spanish-language newspaper out loud every day in front of the mirror. Out of my mouth came word formations, rounded O's and rolled R's that were so different from English. Language was a sociology lesson because it taught me that reality had more than one side to it and that it comes in more than one language. The Spanish-language world had just as many words as did the one I was learning about in school. The knowledge of Spanish even helped me to become the English spelling champion in the eighth grade.

Since my grandfather was a rural teacher in his younger years, his lessons on Mexican history and culture could come at any unexpected time. Sometimes, while we sat together in the backyard, he would talk at length about one of his favorite subjects, or his lesson might begin during an oration when all the neighbors were around. His voice resounded with a loud bass timbre.

One day he pointed to my father's Model T, "You see those tires?" I nodded. "Our forefathers." "What do you mean, Grandfather?" The Olmecas, a brilliant group west of Michoacan, he explained, had discovered rubber before Cortez arrived. Neither car nor aeroplane could travel without it. The Mexicans, he told me, had also discovered *chicle* (gum), which later made Mr. Wrigley rich and famous.

What would the world be like without chocolate, if not for its discovery in Mexico? Even during our dire straits, somehow we managed to make a delicious brew with brown sugar, cinnamon sticks, goat's milk and chocolate. This and other foods were connecting points to an important past, live evidence that those times matter even to the present moment. That memory was embedded in the use of rubber and *chicle* and in the flavor of chocolate and vanilla, which were discovered in and exported to the world from the area of Mexico that became Veracruz.

My ancestors, he said, had made dikes to control the flow of water. Their astronomy enabled them to chart time as accurately as Europe's Julian calendar. A metal facsimile of the great stone Aztec calendar was one of our cherished possessions. One day I took it to school for a "something old, something new" contest, a little like show and tell. My teacher looked at it, puzzled; it was totally meaningless to her. She, in turn, surprised me, for I thought she should have known what it represented. I concluded that I knew a lot more than she about Mexican history because of the teachings of my Grandfather. Unfortunately, I was right.

My grandfather had a knack for simplifying historical facts and injecting vivid color and human feeling into his accounts. He would talk about how the Toltecs, later followed by the Aztecs, made Tenochtitlán one of the largest cities in the world, five centuries before Cortez's coming. He often told us, even while resting from our walnut picking, about the wondrous achievements of the Tarascans, my direct ancestors, who, together with the Mayas, formed great Mesoamerican civilizations before contact with Europeans. As tired as I was, my spirits were lifted at each retelling, and I would sit up with pride.

It was hard for me to accept that so many U. S. educators would be so unaware of Indian civilizations and so unresponsive to the evidence close at hand. After all, if we learned that Egyptian pyramid builders had created a wonder of the world, wouldn't we be equally proud to learn that the largest pyramid on earth was not located in Egypt but in Cholula, in the Mexican state of Puebla? And what surprised me most was that this kind of knowledge was rejected, as if it were not worth knowing. I couldn't understand it. Our teachers really didn't care. Our teachers lacked the imagination and the intellectual curiosity to make the connection. Perhaps the sources seemed beneath credibility.

Their views differed from my grandfather's, who was impatient for us to learn everything we could. He was so eager, he would plan special lessons for us, often making dioramas, physical models, to use in his backyard lectures. He was very gifted, often making life-like figurines and representations of places and events, such as an erupting volcano. His craftsmanship extended beyond dioramas to making bird cages out of redwood taken from redwood ties from the tracks that he painted bright colors, often yellow and green.

When I was eleven, I began to follow his example, but instead of crafts, I took up art through a cartooning correspondence course from the Landon Art School in Cincinnati. I did the assignments inside the Model-T studio. I wanted to be a cartoonist and soon found out that even cartoonists needed more than just inspiration for their creations. The art school's assignments included exercises, such as asking me to draw something I thought was funny. I would send in my work and an artist back in Cincinnati would review and correct what I did. Sometimes, they asked me to do it over and over again. But that was how you learned to become an illustrator, or anything else for that matter, through practice and coaching. Eventually, I had to quit sending in the assignments when the lessons grew too advanced and I couldn't afford the materials. I didn't have the money to buy India ink to do the assignments sent in the mail. That was still during the Depression. In a way, we had been in a depression all along. It's just that when the Depression came along for everyone else, conditions only got worse for us.

One of the countless unsavory experiences at grammar school occurred during lunch hour one day. The Mexican kids would hide to eat because we were embarrassed to take out our burritos in front of the Anglo students. So, everyday we would go into a barn to a loft over the stables where the horses were kept that some kids from the outlying ranches rode to school. We would rather eat there, with smelly manure than have the other children make fun of our food.

We would climb up into the loft and munch away at our burritos. Our families couldn't afford sandwiches with cuts of bologna, pressed ham and other meats or cheese and things like that. Our burritos were plain. They consisted of flour tortillas and beans. Sometimes one of the kids would bring a tasteless burrito with only rice filling. Just for variety and out of fraternal consideration, we would exchange. My mother was such a good cook, my burritos were favorites to trade with because she added a little hot sauce and other spices to them.

The biggest distinction between the Anglo students and us was that they wore shoes and we didn't. The bottoms of our feet were like leather, but even that had its advantages. We could roam the hills and walk over jagged rocks and burrs and thorns from thistle on the ground with my dog, a slingshot and a BB gun. I would spend hours and hours in the hills with Barbón. He would never let me go up into those hills by myself. He was always protective once we got into the back country and any time he sensed danger. Rattlesnake warnings were his specialty.

We couldn't afford to feed him at home because we had enough trouble finding food for ourselves. When my father brought home some over-ripe bananas, partly spoiled, Barbón would eat them. My mother would remind me to feed him the dark, soft parts and keep the good parts of the bananas for ourselves. Sometimes she had me feed him the wilted leaves of lettuce grown in our backyard, but she reminded me to smear some *manteca* (lard) on them. That was Barbón's dog food during the Depression: bananas, lettuce and *manteca*. He was the first vegetarian dog I ever met. Everyone suffered, no one ate well; man and best friend were all forced to adapt.

Sunshine and Rain in Walnut County

Nothing matched the entertainment that Walnut Canyon provided—its cliffs, the panoramic views from the top of the mesa and the often dry stream that ran behind our property. It was our "private" wilderness that transported the imagination to its limits: an unfailing adventure, a supply of surprises and continuous lessons about the effects of terrain and weather on the ambitions humans called "progress."

Some pepper trees grew up there in the hills. The landscape was dry, with dark shadows forming around the trees, brush and rocks. Clustered in places were century plants and cacti with sharp needles. We knew where every patch was and how to navigate around it.

The dry thistle covered with burrs, the cactus with bright red prickly pears and other succulents made up the patchwork of dense vegetation. Yellow, dry grasses covered much of the barren ground like straw. Some eucalyptus trees provided shade.

From the very top of the mesa, you could see the opposite cliff and the rooftops of houses along the rise by the road as well as grain storage at the edge of town. You could see the whole world below and beyond. The Tehachapi Mountains rose above the brown and dull-green hills on the northern horizon and ran south. Over the lowland hills there were patches of trees and green pasturelands, some houses and ranch settlements. The coastal range to the west seemed to rise from the south along a jagged edge until it came to the rich green- and black-colored high rolling hills that contrasted sharply with the deep blue sky in the mid-morning sunlight. Walnut Canyon seemed to be the center of the earth.

While our hill was not the highest, it had the best view of the surrounding territory. It was there, in my solitude, that I learned some of the deepest lessons of my life. Some of my best adventures took place there as well as some of my choicest pranks. The other kids from the canyon and I would have air battles with kites up at the top of the hill by putting razor blades on them to see who was the most skilled in bringing the other ones down. We would spend long afternoons on our backs, watching cloud formations and daydreaming.

When we became a bit older, around thirteen or fourteen, we shifted from nature observers to social commentators. We had a great view from up there of the outhouses. We always had ridiculous things to say about the girls, especially the pretty ones, who went in and out.

In March, 1928, when I was in fifth grade, the St. Francis Dam washed out.

A wall of raging water fifty feet high rushed down the Santa Clara River from the San Francisquito damsite through Santa Paula and Fillmore to the sea near Oxnard. Almost five hundred county residents lost their lives in that disaster. Nineteen bodies were taken to Tanner's Garage, and twenty-two to the back of Whitaker's Hardware Store in our hometown to be washed off for burial.

My father was hired to look for bodies. He enlisted about twelve searchers, who found bodies in the orchards and hauled them out from remote and unlikely places for more than two days. In Fillmore, which took the brunt of the catastrophe, some corpses were found on top of citrus trees, caught there when they were swept away by the rampaging flood. After the water receded, many other remains were found, some partially buried in the mud. They were mostly Mexican families. After they were cleaned up for identification, the county coroner's office sent an assistant to embalm them.

The day before the flood, hundreds of cars streamed past our little home in Walnut Canyon. My family and neighbors were puzzled by the unusually heavy traffic. They had not heard of the evacuation orders that had been given to residents just over the Fillmore Pass.

Although the flood did not hit Moorpark directly, the heavy rain still did its damage, and school was dismissed for a time. Mrs. Mabel Bradley worked the switchboard long and hard, answering long-distance calls from relatives wanting to know about their kin. Only Grimes Canyon Road, three miles away from Walnut Canyon, remained open during the flood.

We knew about floods. Our area flooded often, even though we were on a steep grade. Each time the creek behind our property, a runoff for mountain streams, overflowed, it marked the beginning of disaster.

The makeshift tent we lived in had no foundation or floor. Every time the creek overflowed, soon after the heavy rains began, the tent floor flooded. In 1928, still unaware of the disastrous flooding that was costing many lives, Socorro, Trini and I floated homemade boats in the water from our beds.

One night, while we stood outside in the rain, huddled under a walnut tree, my mother gave birth to my sister, Elvira.

Everyone suffered from the wind and the rain. None of our neighbors were much better off than we were, and that wasn't much better than living under a tree. Sanitation was virtually non-existent. When the outhouses overflowed with the flooding, flies swarmed around the stench that filled the vicinity. The unsanitary conditions made me dread the daily calls of nature.

Dark Days

We were living in the tent when the Great Depression began. It was evident how hard my father was having to work to make payments on the property. He went to work with one rancher after another. As the prices of products plunged, employers couldn't pay him anymore or could only afford to hire him part-time. So he worked for as many ranchers as he could at once, but he mainly alternated between the Wicks, Strathern and Gisler ranches, depending on the crop and the season. When the work played out, he concentrated on his own garden and the little livestock we had that fed us.

During the Depression's darkest days, New York's Mayor Fiorello LaGuardia's voice would come into our tent over the radio. During a newspaper strike, when the comics section of the Sunday paper didn't get out and many couldn't afford a dime for a Sunday paper, he read the funnies over the air. Fondly called "The Little Flower," he helped create a notion that we were all in it together by reading the Sunday comics, the major weekly entertainment for most of us kids. He had a common man's touch and brought a closeness between the kids and the rest of the world, sort of telling them that the society still had some order and everyone was not isolated.

As money disappeared, Chicago gangster Al Capone captured the public imagination, as did the kidnapping by Bruno Richard Hauptman of Charles, "Lucky Lindy", Lindberg's baby in New Jersey. Lindberg's father-in-law, Dwight Morrow, was the United States Ambassador to Mexico who helped negotiate an end to the deadly church-state struggle that had divided Mexico for over a century.

By 1934, the news of John Dillinger's exploits, broadcast over the radio, appeared to outshine even my Grandfather's ability to mesmerize us children with stories. Don Lorenzo kept up with those events as closely as he could through the newspaper that he read carefully, word for word, before passing it on to me. I would read it to practice, and later read it aloud to someone else.

In Mexico during those days, the underlying valor of the people made surprising world news. President Lázaro Cárdenas dared to tell the world's major oil companies, including Britain's and those of the United States, that the subsoil mineral wealth of Mexico, including oil, belonged to the people of Mexico. Foreigners only held usufructory ownership of the oil after it was pumped. He made it stick, and President Roosevelt took no action against Mexico, ignoring the ever eager anti-Mexican jingoes who clamored for the U.S. Marines to be sent to prevent the Mexicans from "stealing" their own oil.

South of the Rio Grande, "Talking Walls," mural paintings, appeared on great public buildings to galvanize Mexico's will to progress. These giant, colorful images proclaimed the determination of the Mexican people to throw off the chains of foreign domination and poverty. Diego Rivera, José Clemente Orozco and David Alfaro Siquieros became household words worldwide as they called for change and condemned evils of past oppressions that had so harshly intruded into the present.

Mexican President Plutarco Elías Calles came to San Diego for medical treatment during my youth. My father would often talk about his much criticized efforts to separate church from state and his championship of Mexico's independence. I was thrilled by the opportunity to accompany my father to San Diego, along with a delegation from throughout Southern California, to visit this great man and shake his hand. It was a moment of living history for me.

After the great Fillmore-Santa Paula flood, the Depression's effect slowly took hold of us, like a contagion. Work became ever more scarce and my father had an increasingly hard time. As young as we were, we were not fully aware of what all this meant. We had never had much to lose, so we didn't miss a lot. We didn't have enough to eat and we noticed that our parents worried more, but that was not unusual. The hill behind Walnut Canyon was still there; many adventures awaited us.

Some of us liked going up the road to play marbles in front of Percy Wicks' house. He didn't pay much attention to us and didn't say much when he saw us. He had his own problems as head of the Walnut Growers Association. He actually seemed amused and often offered us a banana or an apple when he saw us in his front yard.

He didn't care much for ranching; his ranch was a hobby to him. Knowing that made it a lot easier when we stole a watermelon from his patch. But by hanging around his house as much as we did, we noticed that the town ladies went in and out of his house a lot. We just thought he was popular at first. As we got a little older, we started to suspect what was happening, especially when one pretty librarian appeared there. At other times, single, lonely women spent increasing amounts of time with him. We sort of knew what was going on and were amused by it.

But what happened next made me grow up fast.

Don Lorenzo's Kite

I suppose that because of the constant motivation I got at home, I was a little different from the other kids. My feelings about the outside world seemed different. While I was unburdening my soul to my grandfather, my young friends were out there competing with each other and having fun. They weren't bothered by the things that bothered me. There were so many activities for them, including woodcarving, building birdhouses, collecting bird eggs and butterflies, collecting flowers in the summer for their families and making kites. I wasn't that creative.

In those days, the kids living in Walnut Canyon learned how to make kites from newspapers, bamboo and string. They competed with each other to see which one flew the highest, stayed up the longest or was the most colorful. After listening to my tales of woe, my grandfather asked if I had ever seen a Tarascan kite. Naturally, I said no. Tarascan kites, he said, were unlike all the others in the world. Flying a Tarascan kite, he explained, was to be taken very seriously and could be a rite of passage from disappointment to happier pursuits.

Although I was only nine, he asked me whether I was prepared to make that important change. He so inspired me, that I told him I was ready without hesitation. On that day, he prepared to show me how to make this very colorful and different kite that was to leave such an indelible memory.

First, we gathered up all the materials we would need, including dried goat bladder strips and bamboo. Then, he put two large sheets of pink butcher's paper together and pasted the edges with a paste that he made out of flour and water. He explained that the kite needed to be light to get some lift, but strong enough to resist the gusting wind.

When we were finished, the kite had a very unusual shape. It was rectangular and asymmetrical because of the dried goat bladder that he used to tie the two ends in the form of a bow. To me it was beautiful. We had made this marvelous and magical kite. So, we took it up to the top of the canyon to fly it. It was a giant among kites, six feet high and four feet wide.

There, high up over the canyon, my grandfather had me launch it when a strong wind came up, but it didn't fly like the others. It's bright colored streamers shot straight up with such a force that it took all my strength to hold onto the kite. I thought it was going to take me with it as it shot up into the sky.

When that Tarascan kite reached its zenith, taking all the twine we had to give it, we both had to hold on to it so it wouldn't get away from us. We finally tied it to a tree. The kite loomed overhead like a huge, colorful bird in the sky, hovering over the valley from the canyon. Gracefully, like a hawk, it glided from one hilltop to another. Like the sound of a giant viola or the drone of an airplane, the kite issued a roar created by the vibration of the taut goat bladder. Everyone on the hilltop and some people down below stopped to gaze at it in awe. No one had ever seen anything like it. More and more kids gathered around to look at it in amazement.

The next time we flew our unique kite from the top of the hill behind our property, a wind came up and overpowered it, driving it to crash to the ground. Before going down, however, it took giant sweeps skyward, roaring louder than ever. As I lost my grip on the string, I somehow knew that its time had come, but not before it had done the job for which it had been built. Don Lorenzo's kite had been so spectacular that the other kids talked about it for weeks afterwards. It even got written up in our town's newspaper, the *Moorpark Enterprise.*

Watching Don Lorenzo make the kite had taught me a valuable lesson. I learned that thinking through what needs to be done is the first important step in all that we attempt to do. I learned that, like my father and grandfather, I needed to proceed with the same determination and fervor that they demonstrated whenever they did anything. I learned that the construction had to have a solid foundation, not based only on proven materials, but also on traditions. And, finally, that while the trajectory might be unconventional, it could also be swift and colorful. That's what I learned that day at the top of Walnut Canyon—a lesson about what it took to soar to the top of the world, like a Tarascan kite. It was a lesson I never forgot. I was more convinced than ever that my grandfather was a really wise man.

Socorro

My maternal grandfather was a tall, thin man who worked as a shoemaker. He also made other leather goods. I was almost nine when he died of tuberculosis, a disease that was to claim the lives of many of our family members. After his passing, my grandmother Doña Rosa became more zealous about making remedies and preparations for the sick and the injured. She kept a large supply of jars filled with the herbs and homemade medications that she used to treat people for many ailments. Her more popular medications included *ojo de ratón, estafiate, ruda, yerba buena* and *flor del sauco*. As you walked into my grandmother's consulting room and medicine closet, you would be overcome by the overpowering fragrance of rosemary. It never failed to depress us because the scent of rosemary was ever present at the home funerals, which we were, sadly, so used to attending.

Those who were superstitious by nature thought Doña Rosa possessed supernatural powers, which she encouraged by making strange noises reminiscent of native chants and prayers. Two of my buddies and I would sneak in under the porch and watch her as she "washed" away their disease by waving a bouquet of flowers over her patients before giving them her herbal brews.

Before she had left Mexico during the Revolution, she had worked as a nurse's aid at a hospital in León. Recruited first by the Villistas and then by the Obregonistas, she had tended to the wounded soldiers. She assisted doctors in amputating limbs and even helped to bury the dead. She was good at tending to the ill and wounded and seemed to have a genuine talent for helping the soldiers recover quickly. To add to her knowledge, Doña Rosa read extensively about remedies and cures and kept a lot of texts and other books around, especially those written by herbalists, naturalists and homeopaths. Aware that her medicine had its limitations, she would describe some illnesses as, *"fuera del alcance,"* beyond her curative powers.

Doña Rosa was encouraged by her early successes, after applying remedies and using them to help my aunts Santos, Florencia and Ijinia, who had settled in with their husbands in their new households and were raising their families. Before long, Doña Rosa became known as a *curandera*, a folk healer. Most people considered her better than Dr. Frank A. Yoakum, our Moorpark doctor, who was the only physician in the area for many years.

Dr. Yoakum owned the building where Whitaker Hardware was located. In partnership with C. M. Walling, the two had a deal to sell caskets from the back of the hardware store, which served as a showroom. At that time, the eastern part of the county had no morticians. The only communities in the county that had undertakers were Oxnard and Ventura, but Santa Susana, Simi, Thousand Oaks, Newberry Park, Camarillo and Moorpark had none. Since many babies were stillborn, morticians customarily visited the homes to make the burial arrangements.

As far as we knew, Yoakum was the doctor to call on only when the patient had money in hand. Otherwise, most people had to go without care or fend for themselves. Some people who couldn't afford a doctor appealed to my grandmother for help, and she did what she could to the extent of her knowledge and experience. People who had gone to Dr. Yoakum for help, and for whom he said nothing could be done, often ended up going to Doña Rosa as a last resort. She was often able to help them. On Saturdays and Sundays, you could see dozens of people waiting in a line outside her house to seek the advice of this *curandera* who had gained much notoriety around the Moorpark area because of her unconventional cures.

My grandmother's folk medicine might not have been scientifically validated, but she provided it generously and with a concern for the patient's financial means. After being treated, her patients usually came back and paid her with pigs, little goats or lambs. After Don Anastacio died, Doña Rosa supported herself with the offerings made by people she treated and often cured. She never asked them directly for money. Doña Rosa was a healthy, vibrant woman who even outlived her little adobe house, which was torn down in the late 1940s following an earthquake that made it unsafe for habitation.

As I stated earlier, the 1929 economic crash that marked the beginning of the Great Depression occurred at a time when we were still living in the tent and my parents were saddled with the payments my father was making on the Walnut Canyon property. We had no alternative but to set-tle into that shelter with its corrugated tin kitchen for the long haul. A wooden door separated the tent from the kitchen with its woodburning stove that served as the only source of heat for the entire shelter. That wood stove's warmth may have protected my health for what was to hap-pen later.

Even though the tent was very large, there were more of us each year as our family kept growing and my brothers and sisters were born. Consequently, there was no room for me in the main part of the tent. I had to sleep on the dirt floor next to that old stove, for which I considered myself very fortunate during those cold winter nights.

One summer day, while all the family was working in the apricot fields, the lean-to kitchen caught fire and burned down. It was my good fortune it didn't happen at night, or I would have been a goner. I lost some of my important child-hood treasures like my marbles, BB gun and slingshot, but more important, perhaps, my favorite sleeping place.

During this period, my father found it very difficult to support us from his limited income from working for Percy Wicks in the summer and the Gislers at other times. The stress of trying to support his family and save the money for his property was very demanding and often caused friction between the adults.

My mother felt deeply hurt at having to play second fid-dle to my grandmother. The preferential treatment given my father and the slights to my mother drove a wedge between my parents. At the same time, everyone struggled just to get by under difficult circumstances. From my mother's point of view, my father had a right to show favoritism to his par-ents, but not at the expense of his own family. Doña Hilaria, on the other hand, played it up in light of my mother's apparent vulnerability.

My little sister, Socorro, was outspoken about my grand-mother's behavior toward our mother. In no uncertain terms, she always defended my mother against my grand-mother's criticism of her. Socorro was a gifted child who did well in school, made friends easily and was very popular with her classmates. She was small and delicate and very pretty. I was two years older than Socorro when she became ill at the age of ten. After taking the *estafiate* herb my mother gave her during her illness, Socorro seemed to recover. And after regaining her strength, she ran around and played as she normally did. It appeared that the healing brew my mother had given her was all she needed.

Sometimes, in the middle of the night, I would climb the hill behind our property to look for the *estafiate* when my mother needed it to medicate Socorro. *Estafiate* was the remedy my mother instinctively resorted to whenever any of us became ill. It was the same remedy that seemingly kept Ijinia alive and had even revived her when she and my mother were stranded in Arizona. I had more *estafiate* poured into me than any other remedy or medicine in my life—more than my brothers and sisters—because I was the oldest and had been through more bouts of illness than they had. Maybe that's why I survived.

Socorro, however, became ill again and this time it seemed even my mother's precious herbs could not heal her. At first, when she started getting sick again, Socorro still played outside with the rest of us. In time, she lost her strength and she just couldn't seem to regain it as quickly as she had before.

My sister's illness began with a hacking cough that wouldn't stop. Then, her symptoms worsened and she got diarrhea that gradually dehydrated her tiny body. We stood by, helplessly watching her shrivel into a living skeleton. Her large brown eyes bulged as her once beautiful face became smaller and turned brownish red from the uncontrollable fever that tormented her.

At first, her treatment was entirely in my mother's and Doña Rosa's capable hands. To help her feel better, they gave Socorro the *estafiate* from the plants I found in the hills behind the tent. Then, they started giving her what seemed like a hundred bottles of Pulmotol, a widely publicized cough medicine of the day. But no remedy seemed to work, and Socorro continued to grow weaker.

My grandmother decided Socorro needed some other remedy, something more powerful and magical. Doña Rosa placed a dead chicken over Socorro's stomach and left it there to decompose. She believed the common folk myth that the dead animal would suck the illness out of my sister's frail body. At the end of four days, I removed the foul-smelling carcass. The stench was so strong, it made me gag when I disposed of it.

Throughout Socorro's ordeal, my mother made us pray for her every night while she lay ill just a few feet from where we slept. Everything seemed so barren. I discovered for the first time that life can feel as dry as dust. Not even God seemed to hear us. Our petitions weren't helping. Socorro's condition only worsened.

Although we couldn't afford it, my father couldn't just let her die. We sold three goats and finally got a doctor, a wiry mouse of a man, to come and look at her. Relieved that Socorro was now in the doctor's hands, my father told us not to worry. He honestly believed that now, with proper attention, our beloved Socorro would soon get well. But every time the doctor, in whom my father had so much confidence, made a house call, he would take her temperature and pulse, then recommend only cough medicine and some pills. All he did was look at this once beautiful child whose life was slipping away. He never even offered a diagnosis of her illness. But he did insist on getting paid five gold dollars for every visit! What that doctor wanted, the only value we were to him, was his final $100 fee for the cumulative home visits. That $100 was a fortune to us. The only hand he extended was for whatever he could get. To him it was $100. For us, it was Socorro's life.

Even to this day, I find it difficult to forgive him for not trying harder to save her. Deep down, I would harbor a resentment that had she not had such dark skin, had her name not been Morales, had we lived on the other side of the tracks or been people of some social standing, Socorro might have lived. With financial means, we might have been able to take her to a proper hospital where a lung x-ray could have been taken and she could have been treated by competent specialists, and her life could have been spared.

I loved my sister very much. She was my soul mate. Even though she was younger than I, I always respected the wisdom of her young years and the courageous way she stood up for people when she felt they had been mistreated or ignored. I admired her genius and the beauty that emanated from within her, reaching out to embrace others with her sparkling laughter, her love and her loyalty. She was like a twin to me, and when she died, a part of me died with her.

I still feel the sorrow of her death and my mother's pain as she held her child helplessly in her arms, praying against fading hope that her life might be spared. I have never forgotten the moment when Socorro, cradled in my mother's arms, drew her final breath and died.

I can't describe the grief I felt then. At that moment, my heart told me she had joined the angels in heaven. Then, a sound filled the shelter that I'll never forget. Although I knew the wailing sound was coming from my mother, it sounded foreign to me. It pained me at that moment almost more than my sister's death.

I want to say that it was a mother's soulful cry of pain that escaped from her lips, but it was more than that. It was as if every painful moment she had ever known in her life was in that piercing sound I heard filling the room with unrestrained grief. It was the sound of utter futility and, at that moment, it made me want to die, too.

At first, I thought my mother was trying to coax Socorro back to life, as if that final moment had not already passed, as if she could postpone the moment of death. But life had already whispered to us and left us with only Socorro's memory for all time.

I turned and ran out of the tent, wanting to escape death's visit, wanting to escape the sound of my mother's grief as it followed me outside. With the tears of pain trickling down my face, I ran until I was exhausted. I ended up at a small stream that ran alongside our property. I was so intent on escaping from the pain of my sister's death that I didn't notice that my dog, Barbón, had followed me. As I sat there by the side of the stream, I saw him lying beside me. I don't know how long I sat there, trying to stop the tears, or how long it was before I realized that the screams I heard were no longer my mother's. They were my own. Blinded by anger and rage, I threw rocks into the darkness and cried out loud, angry tears. I pulled weeds and bushes up by their roots. Throughout my ordeal, Barbón remained beside me, whimpering as if, in his own way, he was trying to tell me that he, too, shared my grief and wanted to console me.

Nothing I know explains why some of us endure and others do not, why life for some has to be a trial and for others a holiday. But there is no justice when a child dies. What is life's worth when one of us is taken before completing the life cycle?

Death was a mystery to me. Socorro's illness and subsequent demise came too suddenly and without logic. Another outcome had to have been possible. What could we have done to cure Socorro? Why had no one told us that her disease was tuberculosis? Why hadn't we known what to do?

As we later came to realize, her illness had been a consequence of our malnutrition, our poverty. Tuberculosis would soon become an epidemic that would claim many more lives, and there wasn't anything that anybody—not the schools nor the doctors—could do to stop it.

That incompetent doctor hadn't even told us that Socorro had TB and that it was highly contagious. He advised no steps to protect the family. We didn't even know what TB was and that we had been exposed to it. No one told us to get x-rayed or have our sputum tested.

We had very little when the Depression started, except for high hopes. Our bodies were not prepared to combat the disease that had taken Socorro. In the end, the lack of proper nutrition, horribly unhealthy surroundings and ignorance transformed tuberculosis into a plague. The epidemic of which my sister was but one victim quickly spread throughout the vicinity. Twenty of my relatives died of tuberculosis during the next five years. It's quite possible that my grandfather, Don Anastacio, had unintentionally infected the rest of us with this dreaded disease. After he died, Don Pedro, Santos, Ijinia and Florencia, as well as María Pérez's husband, Gregorio, all died of tuberculosis. They were followed by my cousin, Diego, our friends, Juan Hidalgo, Ricardo Almaguer, Sofía and Juanita Corralejo. Seven of my brothers and sisters also died. Antonia died after Socorro, followed by Petra, Panchita, Ricardo, Pedro and Cuca. Later, in 1942, Trinidad, my younger brother, passed away while a senior in high school. Only Elvira, Tim and I survived the plague that had destroyed the rest of our family.

Diarrhea, coughing and wasting away—all symptoms of tuberculosis—preceded each baby's death. I was there each time my mother held an infant in her arms and that baby drew its last breath. I knew the moment death came. Each time I was tormented by my mother's grieving and the penetrating wail that symbolized the depth of her spiritual wound. Painfully, her grief would become mine. No matter how much I wanted it to go away, the wound never seemed to heal. I was reminded of it time and again, each time a child died.

Then, the Depression unleashed another plague against us. It seemed as though no matter how hard we tried, nothing was working in our favor. It was a different epidemic that had actually begun the year Socorro had died, inflicted upon us by people who wanted us expelled from the country. It was an infectious state of being that threatened to strip us of everything that was meaningful in our lives—our dignity and our rights as human beings. Wholesale deportations, called "repatriation," were sweeping through our communities.

It seemed that matters could not get any worse. Percy Wicks, the Stratherns and the Gislers could no longer provide my father with work. He was not alone. Everywhere we turned, others had lost their jobs, too. Unable to find buyers, the ranchers could not sell their harvests. The economy had collapsed around us.

Time To Go!

My father went without work for a long time. He picked up odd jobs, like cleaning chicken coops for a dozen eggs or raking a barn and getting paid with two gallons of milk. Finally, he was able to get a job as a janitor at Moorpark High School. Highly respected in the community and with good recommendations, he was accepted right after he was interviewed for the job. I acted as translator during the interview. But public attitudes were working against us. As the Depression intensified, a large population of Mexicans, like the society at large, became unemployed. Competition for jobs with "Americans" led to anti-Mexican sentiment and wholesale deportations. Even back then, Mexicans in the Southwest were blamed for the Depression and unemployment in America.

One day, when the local high school found itself short of a janitor, my father happened to show up and put himself right to work as a substitute in the emergency. The principal was pleased and, on June 20, 1928, the sun broke through the clouds for the Morales family. My father accepted the job and signed the notice of employment to be the official janitor of Moorpark High School. His new salary was $900 per year, which was a lot of money by our standards, especially in terms of the gold-standard dollars then in use.

During the first months of 1931, 9,000 immigrants left the Los Angeles area. The county government had set up a budget of $155,000 to finance the exodus, figuring it had saved $695,000 in welfare aid. I don't recall one Mexican family receiving a dime.

Trains left monthly with repatriated passengers, and by December, as many as three trains left per month. In that first year, the *Los Angeles Times* estimated that about 200,000 *"repatriados"* left the United States. Half of them were from the Los Angeles area, many of my Moorpark neighbors among them. Even Ray Tafoya and his family, who lived three houses away, went with high hopes.

My father had worked at Moorpark High School for about a year when he was informed that he had to be dismissed because he was not a U.S. citizen. Regulations, he was told, required that only citizens could hold public jobs. My father sank into a deep personal depression, which later caused him to experience long periods of anger, during which he refused to talk to anyone. He couldn't believe what had happened. He had been doing a good job and was well liked.

The loss of my father's job affected me as well. I was in the eighth grade at the time and I wanted him to keep his job as much as he did. For one thing, our economic situation had improved and, for another, when I would go over to see him at work, I'd take a hot shower in the gym, which made me feel just grand. The closest I had ever come to taking a shower at home was when we took a large MJB coffee can, punched holes in the bottom, nailed it to a walnut tree and tied a hose to it. Two gunny sacks served as a curtain.

My father had heard that the Mexican government had agreed to repatriate people living in Southern California and other parts of the United States. That led him to submit an application to settle in Estero Beach, near Ensenada in Baja California. We were to get a plot of land to farm there. After we received news that his application had been accepted, we began making arrangements to leave.

One of the special trains traveling to Los Angeles passed through Moorpark. We received our instructions, telling us which train we were to take just two days before its scheduled arrival. We, along with everyone else who had been accepted, bustled around, frantically trying to decide what to pack and what to leave behind. There were many preparations to make in a very short time.

The plan was that we would try to homestead in Baja California. Don Lorenzo, Doña Hilaria and the rest of my father's family would re-settle there later. They chose not to leave because someone had to stay behind to look after the property now that it was paid for. And who knew, maybe it wouldn't work out, anyway. Later, if my father could make a farm productive in Baja, perhaps he could sell the land in Walnut Canyon.

A series of misadventures delayed us. There were too many arrangements and belongings to take or dispose of in such a short time. Reflection also delayed us. My father and mother had set out just a dozen years before to find a way out of an impossible situation by migrating north from Guanajuato. Before them, Don Lorenzo and Doña Hilaria had migrated west from Guanajuato's highlands for the same reason. Now, the cycle was beginning all over again, only this time, my parents had American children whose own countrymen were encouraging the exodus. Greed and blame became more important than benevolence and reason in yet another major crisis.

Time itself conspired against us, no matter how fervently my parents worked to gather everything up and get us ready to leave. I wanted to be the last one to leave Walnut Canyon, so I waited as long as possible to get into the car that was to take us to the station. From the rise on the hill, I could hear the train coming from the direction of Santa Barbara and making its way through the pasturelands in the valley toward Moorpark station. I saw it pull up into the station. Frankly, I didn't want to leave my friends that I had known all my life and my dog. We didn't get there in time and the train pulled away from the station without us. My father's loss was my gain.

As the full force of the family's failure to depart for Baja California swept through my father's mind, his face gave dramatic expression to his anger, disappointment and disillusionment. His reaction was sharpened by the fact that he had already received a paper of commitment from Ventura County for a plot of agricultural land at Estero Beach, just south of Ensenada.

Although reluctant at the thought of leaving Moorpark, the new adventure had caught my imagination. How wonderful it would be to live in a home near the beach! My father had passed his days dreaming of his farm at Estero and talking continuously of all the tomatoes he would grow there.

While many in the crowd who were left at the station made light of the situation, when the southbound train pulled out joking and laughing at their dilemma, my father showed no signs of seeing any humor in the matter.

In the meantime, there were the dramatic preparations being made by the Tafoya family. They weren't in the least concerned with the matter of the train. If I recall correctly, their family had another way of getting to the free farmland in Baja. They would travel in their new Model T Ford truck. My father, having missed the train (and having wrecked his own Model T months earlier), went to see whether his family, too, could ride on the well-loaded Model T.

I suppose Norman Rockwell could have made a memorable picture out of the sight of little me, looking up into the faces of the head of the Tafoya family and my father as they discussed the remote possibility that our family could ride south in the Model T, too. What a negotiation—Raycel Tafoya, the head of the family, with his big cigar and his determined refusal, and my father, who tried to soften his friend up with the gift of our little Philco radio.

Raycel Tafoya said, "No." He explained that he had to leave room to load the farm equipment he planned to pick up in San Diego. There would be no room for the Morales family.

There was and is a piece of irony in the well-laid plans of the Tafoyas to move their whole family to free land in Mexico. They were not Mexicans! They were all native-born Americans of Mexican heritage. They had all been born in Arizona.

Six months later, the whole Tafoya family returned to Moorpark, having abandoned their "free land" venture at Estero! The explanation for the abandonment of the Estero land by many repatriated Mexicans boiled down to one main cause: they had been unable to understand or adapt to the unfamiliar cultural and legal differences in Baja, California. Ironically, they turned out to be frustrated immigrants from another land with an Anglo-dominated tradition.

⸻

Our situation was desperate. My father needed to come up with a solution quickly. Food, like money, was scarce. I don't recall ever eating so much goat meat and chicken soup. The vegetables we raised in our back yard were distributed through family ties and bartering. When someone killed a pig, everyone around Walnut Canyon had an uncanny way of finding out about it. That was about the time people would come around to collect a debt and receive payment for the loan or favor with a few pounds of *"carnitas,"* some chops, fat for cooking, the outer layer of skin for frying and even the feet to flavor *menudo.* Every part of the animal was used and distributed. Someone always needed or wanted each part—the jowls, picnic shoulders, hocks, belly, butt ham, hind foot, hind loin and fat back. Sausage was made from the blood. Similarly, rabbits and chickens were traded like cash. Had there not been a barter system, there would have been no economy in Walnut Canyon.

People looked out for each other whether they were kin or friends. No one stole anything from the other and there was no crime. No one was confused in the immigrant community about what they were up to. They had all come to work. Families would meet by the dim light of a kerosene lantern to discuss this dilemma—no jobs. That was the one possession that everyone wanted and no amount of bartering could get them. My father's problem was that he needed to get his hands on some commodities to trade in order to build his own economy.

Having learned the practical side of supply and demand by trading soap in Guanajuato, he had a merchant's instincts. Now, he applied those same principles to our situation. He started going to the Los Angeles produce market, where he picked up fruits and vegetables for which he would pay something minimal, only a dollar or so. Much of it was not fancy packed or of the highest grade. So, he bought food at discount prices and succeeded in making a profit in reselling it. He knew the merchant's business axiom—successful buying leads to successful selling—and he knew how to buy.

My father took the produce back to Moorpark, where he set up a fruit stand. There, I learned from my father that an attractive display of fruits and vegetables was the key to making money. None of the fruit he bought was wasted, because he would bring home what he didn't sell at the stand. We divided the shrunken apples and other fruit that had over-ripened. Our cat ate spoiled oranges and the dog was fed rotten bananas. Everybody had to eat fruit if they didn't want to die. The cat and dog were somewhat reluctant, but not adamant.

Our economic recovery began when my father returned to the ways of the merchant. His produce stand became quite popular. A lot of people started gathering around it to pass the time of day. It was a colorful setting, like the old country cracker barrel store, but with a Mexican flavor. Anything that happened in town—a wedding, a job opportunity, a death—hit there first, which added to my father's role as an advocate. As business improved, he took down the red canvas roof he was using and built a roof. The stand eventually became a small grocery store. After that, he quickly raised the money to build the house he had wanted from the beginning. If only Socorro had lived to see it.

My father became good friends with the constable, the sheriff and the district attorney. One day, my father reported a burglary at his store to the sheriff, who quickly found three tents full of stolen goods and asked my father to go out and identify his property. He had me drive him in his new Chevrolet truck to the ranch where the sheriff was waiting for him. I did not understand why we needed a three-ton truck, because nothing had been stolen but gum and candies, but he insisted we take it. When we arrived, we found the tents filled with radios, furniture, household items, soda water and even watches and clocks.

"Tell your father to take whatever is yours," the sheriff said. I translated the instruction and my father said, "Tell the sheriff that it's all mine. In fact, there are even some items missing." Of course, that wasn't true. We didn't sell watches or radios. The fact of the matter was that we did quite well after I loaded the truck up and he sold the merchandise. This brings up one of the contradictions in his character; the kind of inconsistency, I guess, that many of us share.

This wasn't the first time that our store had been broken into. In fact, it happened a number of times. Although it appeared sturdy with its red Mexican tile roof, it was also isolated on the outskirts of town. One time, he found someone stealing inside the store when he opened up in the morning. The burglar ran out and jumped on my father's plow horse to get away. My father chased him by jumping on his other plow horse, without a saddle. He grabbed his .45 and galloped down the street and into a field right on the tail of the thief at a fast pace. My father took aim and fired. Down went the thief's horse. The incident and subsequent arrest made the headlines in the *Moorpark Enterprise*. I have often thought that it could have made a good scene in a cowboy movie.

As a youth, I was kept busy with helping out at our store. When the families came from Los Angeles and the surrounding towns to work the harvests, Dad had me go around the camps and take grocery orders. Many of the families didn't have money, but he extended credit until payday. At first, I didn't do well. I complained that I just wasn't cut out to be a successful salesman.

In his most assertive manner, he would often repeat, "You have to learn that a man's downfall comes from *no se puede, puede ser, ahi veremos, quién sabe, qué dirán*." These phrases were unacceptable: "It can't be done, maybe, we'll see, who knows, what will they say." He would reflect a second, then add, *"Y usted nunca está muy ocupado*—And you're never too busy." All ready-made excuses were flimsy, and none were new, original or good enough, he insisted.

Once we moved into the house my father built for us, our lives were changed. Now the family was eager to succeed. I was growing and soon it would be time for me to enroll in high school. That would turn out to be a story in itself, another plateau in a strange world.

Painful Indignities

It was during my years in high school that I became acutely aware of the rejection and isolation that we had to endure in predominately Anglo schools. I had begun to feel the uncomfortable climate in grammar school when Mr. Robert Carmichael, the school principal, separated the Anglo kids from the Mexicans under the guise of forming teams during recess. At the time, I didn't understand exactly why, but it was beginning to dawn on me that it might all be because we looked different. But attitudes like Mr. Carmichael's made me feel that no matter what we did or how good we were, we would always be just those "Mexican kids."

When I started high school in 1932, my old school mates were suddenly gone. I was abruptly surrounded by only Anglo children and blond, blue-eyed teachers. Yet, my high school was only one block away from Walnut Canyon. Still coping with a heavy accent, on top of everything else, I found myself walking the school hallways alone. Quickly, I had to adapt to being left out. In my days at Moorpark High School, it was the expected thing to maintain a none-too-subtle ethnic separation.

I was by no means the only Mexican American student to suffer these painful indignities. But it is never pleasant to personally receive the message, veiled or brash, that one is not really welcome. Perhaps the full effect of these attitudes on my pride as a high school student was somewhat masked. The eagerness with which I attempted to become involved in extra curricular activities helped me feel more included. I liked music enough to pay the price of long and ardent practice. I was determined to learn to play the trumpet well.

There were no idle instruments in our home other than an old mandolin. But our barber displayed in his downtown shop a nice silver trumpet that was for sale. It shined like something I could never hope to own. I saw it and desired it more every time I got my hair cut. Anyway, my father yielded to my ceaseless nagging and bought the trumpet for me.

By my sophomore year, I had become adept enough to play first trumpet in the Moorpark High School Band. I could read music well. My part in our band did much to alleviate my feelings of being left out. After all, I had not begged to join, but had actually been recruited. It's really not surprising, because good trumpet players were by no means plentiful in the Moorpark of the 1930s. How proud I was! Finally, I was part of something!

But, it was not long before my excitement at being accepted as a musician was to be overshadowed by the trauma of exclusion. The incident stands out in a wide memory of horrendous experiences. It left one more permanent scar on me.

It all started as a field trip designed to please a high school student like me. Our school dance band, which I had also joined, was bussed to the popular Ocean Park Dance Pavilion to hear Henry Busey, the famous trumpet player, and his band. On the Friday evening of our arrival, the teacher lined us up to buy our tickets for the event. But when it came my turn to buy a ticket, the cashier told my teacher that Mexicans were not admitted to the Ocean Park Pavilion. The teacher simply went in with my fellow band members and told me that I was to wait outside until the group came out.

The pier was cold and windy. The misty wind from the ocean went right through my flimsy clothes. My only black suit and gray felt hat offered no comfort. I sat on that pier alone on a cold wet bench for three hours and silently wept inside.

I had befriended our saxophone player, George Caswell, who came out to see what had happened to me. He was deeply shocked at what I told him and offered to buy me a ticket. But he too was refused, because the ticket was obviously for me. Then, another blow fell. I told the cashier that I did not want to dance, but only wished to listen to the music. I was willing to sit behind the curtain where I could see and hear. The scornful expression which accompanied my rejection made me more angry than humiliated.

Here I had come all the way from Moorpark to Ocean Park to hear Henry Busey. He was the trumpeter with the catchy style who had popularized "When Day Is Done." I idolized him. I wanted to sound like him someday, even though I had already somehow begun to develop a folksier, Mexican style in a trio I had formed to play at parties.

Of course, Mr. Busey could not possibly have known about a broken-hearted young fan who wanted so desperately to meet him. Instead, Mr. Busey's devoted young admirer, who collected his records in far away Moorpark, sat out on the cold, dark pier alone, waiting in misery and disappointment for the long, sad ride home.

It was bad enough to be excluded by the Pavilion because I was "Mexican," but what hurt and confused me even more was the fact that my teacher, the very one who encouraged me to come along on this field trip, seemed to care little about my well-being. Would it have required a lot of effort to suggest that I might wait in the bus, where it was warm?

Finally, after all that, something good happened. I eventually acquired all of Henry Busey's records, since I really wanted my trumpet playing to be as good as his. After practicing for a long time, it appeared that my efforts had paid off. In my senior year, our principal appointed me Musical Valedictorian for our Class of '37.

What an honor for me. I didn't have to make a speech, but I did play my trumpet for the graduating class, ironically, right on the stage of the El Rancho Theater, where Mexicans were not allowed to sit in the middle section. It was a tremendous reward after having gone through so much discrimination for so long. It was an unparalleled moment of excitement. I was so proud to invite all my relatives to attend. There was, however, to be a sad letdown. My father, whose approval was always so important to me, adamantly refused to attend, because he was still bitter and angry over the segregation of our people and others in that theater. He couldn't bring himself to sit there and watch me perform, knowing full well that the consensus of the people assembled in the auditorium was still tainted by anti-Mexican feelings. What should have been one of my shining moments was clouded by this irony.

When the graduation ceremony began, I walked up and took my place under the hot lights and began to play. At that moment, I was so nervous I felt as if everyone could see my heart pounding. But I did so well that, suddenly, the first glimmer of self-esteem surfaced. It was the tip of a new feeling. I was on cloud nine when I looked across the audience and saw everyone giving me a standing ovation. And there was my mother in the first row, not in that damnable segregated section, standing and clapping with the others.

It was Jane Wilson, my piano accompanist, and I who shared that moment of unequaled emotion. I thanked the Virgin of Guadalupe for giving me the strength and ability to finally give me a taste of what I always knew I wanted to feel, a little bit of pride.

My desire to belong never left me. But whenever I went to out-of-town football games to cheer my Moorpark High "Musketeers" and got on the bus for these trips, it was seldom that any of my fellow students showed any desire to sit with me. And I remember when I played basketball, a fellow student among the fans, the son of a Norwegian immigrant himself, shouted out in front of all the crowd, "There goes that dirty brown devil again." That remark, of course, was directed at me in front of all my friends and the entire crowd.

Again, during my pursuit of music I would be deeply humiliated. I had been invited to sing in an operetta. My music teacher thought I had a good voice, and so I went to two or three rehearsals. But any glory I might have felt at that time was ruined by the comments of some of my schoolmates—made with the intention of being heard. They questioned whether anyone with dark brown skin should have the "gall" to be in an operetta.

I cannot ever with good conscience accuse our principal of not accepting me personally. He was convinced that Mexicans definitely had their place and should be proud to keep it. To him, it was a simple matter of "your people" versus "our people." When five universities, including UCLA and USC, sent their recruiting teams to our high school, I was deliberately omitted from the interviews. They never told me about them; they just left me sitting there. My angry father, in limited but forceful English, protested to the principal, who simply responded, "Who is going to pick the crops if I encourage your people to go to college?"

English Only vs. Se Habla Español

I lived through the days when the idea of "English only" was imposed on children in school by force. Children were punished during my school years for speaking Spanish—even on the playgrounds at recess. Every time I was caught speaking Spanish, I would be taken to the principal's office. She would then wash my mouth out with soap at an old, rusty, tin bathtub. The bitter taste of soap and water, shoved into my mouth by the teacher while she held my head down, made me feel as if I were drowning. The experience is ingrained in my memory. I started getting my mouth washed out when I was only six years old. It was an unbelievably vicious way to try to cleanse me not only of my family language and culture, but also the language of my community. Today, I would be jailed if I did what they did to me to the pre-schoolers in the centers I administer. Yet, there is little difference between many of these children and the child that I was.

I can remember every summer taking a shopping trip with my family to Los Angeles from far-off Simi Valley to buy clothes for us. My father would drive us over the Santa Susana Pass, across the dry San Fernando Valley and into downtown Los Angeles. He would park on Main Street and shop in the nearest store that announced, *"¡Aquí se habla español!"* There, we would buy our clothes for the coming year, spending all the cash we had saved for the big occasion.

In those days, we shopped where our family's language was understood and spoken. Now, seventy years later, the corporate world, which has plenty to sell us, is careful to do much of its advertising in the language of our heritage.

Later, when I worked for the Department of Labor, I went to a labor camp in Los Baños and spoke to the workers in Spanish. The foreman shouted in a debasing manner, "Speak English." Rather than go into the obvious fact that the workers didn't speak English, I retorted, "All these workers just got here from Mexico. And, after all, we're in California, aren't we?"

I then attempted to give him a lesson in California history by saying that the name "California" itself derived from a Spanish novel of the mid-sixteenth century which spoke of Queen Calafia and her mythical island of California.

He said, "We're in the United States, speak English."

I continued, "Are you insisting that we change Los Baños to 'Bathroom,' California?"

I underwent a similar confrontation in Atascadero, California. In a conference that would hopefully allow me to train ex-offenders to work in the outside world, I again got into a needless, high-pitched argument with one of the administrators when I spoke to the inmates in Spanish.

"We don't speak Spanish around here," he said in a derogatory tone.

Sarcastically, I responded, "Okay, if you want to be technical, I will refer to Atascadero as 'Mudhole,' California, hereafter."

City of Contrasts

I had agreed with my father's advice and rejected my high school principal's admonition against going to college. I chose Santa Barbara State Teacher's College (later to become the University of California at Santa Barbara). With the formal blessing of my mother, I set out for college by train with a $20 bill in my pocket. The "twenty" had been given to me by my father in a farewell gesture. He shook my hand, embraced me and said, *"¡Buena suerte!"* as I climbed on the train.

I doubt, very much whether I could have survived the hassle of college registration had it not been for the savvy and sympathy of the taxi driver who drove me to the campus. I might have walked away from the aggravation and lost a whole semester.

The sympathetic taxi driver discharged me at the head of a long line of eager prospective college registrants. They all appeared to be from well-to-do backgrounds. It was the era of bobby socks and swing music. They turned and stared at me. And there I was in my trim black suit with my bewildered expression, the typical hick from who-knows-what barrio. My natural inclination was to retreat immediately to the end of the waiting line. But my taxi driver mentor grabbed my arm and insisted in a loud voice, "You stand right there!"

It became apparent during my first steps in the registration process that the remainder of my twenty dollar bill would never be enough to pay my fees. Thoughtfully, the college gave me a day of grace to find the additional funds I would need.

Transcripts? I couldn't even spell it, much less find one in my black suit.

"What's your major?" Good Lord, I had always thought a major was an army officer. I shrugged my shoulders and looked puzzled.

"You don't have a major? Then why did you come to Santa Barbara State College?"

At a loss for an instant reply, I mumbled, "I'd sort of like to be an art teacher. I can draw."

That did it. I was referred to the distinguished head of the art department, Mary Croswell. At that moment, little did I know that she would be such a force in the development of my thoughts and plans. She graciously sat with me and helped me choose the proper courses for my first semester. We hit it off well. We immediately began to discuss Mexican art. Fortunately, I had already done considerable reading about and listened to the many colorful stories that my grandfather had told me about how Mexico was recognized as a world art center.

She included one course I'll never forget. It was "Drawing the Human Figure in Charcoal." Here I was, never much out of Walnut Canyon, much less out of Moorpark and in my first week I was attempting to draw a statuesque, naked, blond model! I had never seen bare breasts. Living in Moorpark had never offered me such an opportunity. I never imagined that a woman's breasts could be so imposing. However, I kept my composure. No one ever knew the height that my blood pressure reached that day.

I was overwhelmed to realize that Mary Croswell had taken an interest in me. We had long conversations about Mexican muralists, Diego Rivera, José Clemente Orozco and David Alfaro Siqueiros. I was surprised and thrilled that she was so deeply moved and well-informed about how they addressed the horrors of the working people of Mexico.

With the reticence of a country boy in the presence of such a loving personage as Professor Croswell, I could not bring myself to ask her who, basically, she thought I was. I settled for my own conclusion that she thought of me as a promising foreign student, perhaps from Mexico. She called me "My Dear Señor." I did speak with a slight accent, and she dwelled on her fascination with the wonders of Mexico she had come to love as a traveler.

She made no bones about displaying her favoritism for me, even challenging instructors in her department who dared to give me less than flattering grades.

Every time I was around Mrs. Croswell, I struggled to find the right words to say. In her presence, I was always unsure of myself. She was an attractive, urbane woman. Nevertheless, she treated me as though I were the most important person in her life.

⌒

One of my reasons for choosing Santa Barbara was the whole mystique of that mission city's Spanish heritage and its Mediterranean-style architecture. The city survived on tourism, wealthy retired people and agriculture. Its strawberries, avocados and flowers were famous. Its lemons were known world-wide, even in Russia.

On arriving in 1937, I found Santa Barbara to be a small coastal city of elegance and beauty, built on a narrow shelf of land between the hills and the sea. Just north of the city, where I used to devote hours to perfecting my talents in watercoloring, wind shaped trees overhung high cliffs above the sand. But the rich Spanish atmosphere and the idyllic setting covered another and darker side of life, which would be brought home to me suddenly and without ceremony.

My first day on campus, I was referred to a rooming house run by a Kentucky-bred lady. She was very kind and tried to be helpful. She said, "Look, young man, I couldn't explain renting a room to you to my other tenants. There is a quaint Mexican town in Santa Barbara, down on Haley Street. Why don't you go down there? You'll be happy there. There are lots of cafes that serve your kind of food. You can find a room there."

I took her advice reluctantly, but the message, no matter how kindly put, was loud and clear. This single exchange was a major blow to my making a successful entry into a whole new world. So, I went among "my own people," as the lady from Kentucky had suggested. After countless referrals, I finally found someone who had a room to rent me. There, I got another surprise.

I knocked on a door of a house at the border of the "Mexican quarter." A tall, dignified man, who had been described to me as a distinguished leader of Santa Barbara's Mexican community, came to the door and seemed to look right through me. He resembled the actor, Basil Rathbone. He was hardly distinguishable from the caste-conscious aristocrats who still dominate Mexican society. It felt as though he expected me to start begging for something. He asked what I wanted. I asked him if he had a room to rent. Almost reluctantly, he led me into the living room. Once, his wife came through the room and spoke to him, but acted as though she didn't see me. To her, I was invisible. He showed me a clean, orderly room upstairs, which I accepted. I immediately settled into the room. Later, I was to learn that this man and his family were wealthy people once, but had been driven out of Mexico by President Plutarco Elías Calles. Now they were in such financial ruin that they had to rent rooms in their home. It was obvious to me that Mr. and Mrs. Alfonso Bringas never forgot their caste and color attitudes, so prevalent even today. The disdain and air of superiority with which that faded gentleman of Spanish lineage first surveyed me has never left my memory. I got the impression he was saying with his eyes, "Shouldn't you be at the servant's entrance?" Eventually, he did say to me, "To get to your room, perhaps you should use the back door." During occasional casual conversations, he made no bones about his distaste for anyone with indigenous blood. But his wife and sister-in-law never even spoke to me during the time I lived there. It took me only two weeks to find another place and move.

Racism with a Difference

College opened up a whole new world to me. I began to develop a more sophisticated appreciation of the democratic achievements of my country. I became proud of and learned to rely on the guarantees of freedom in our Constitution and I saw the Supreme Court as the guardian of our individual liberties.

Like a clap of thunder, World War II would invade my academic reverie. Far off, Pearl Harbor had been bombed, and Goleta, only seven miles from my campus, was shelled by a submarine! Then, suddenly, the shock of racism, goaded on by fear-driven hatred, invaded my sheltered college life. It was not directed against Mexicans this time, but toward another well-established California ethnic group—the Japanese.

After Pearl Harbor was bombed on December 7, 1941, California's anti-Japanese groups, including elements of the Native Sons, the American Legion and the California "Joint Immigration Committee" took up the cry of, as they put it, the "Japs must go!" President Franklin D. Roosevelt gave in to the pressure and transferred control of "enemy alien U. S. residents" to the military authorities. The die was cast. Fear and prejudice had won. The hated *Nipponese* did have to go. Leading the hue and cry for exile to the desert for the politically defenseless minority were California Attorney General (later Governor and then Supreme Court Justice) Earl Warren and Los Angeles Mayor Fletcher Bowron. Bowron fulminated against the "Japanese fifth column" over the radio and purged City Hall of all Japanese American municipal employees. General John L. De Witt issued the fateful order that on a certain date, at a certain hour, all people of "Japanese ancestry," natural-born American citizens or not, were to be loaded into trains, buses and trucks for relocation away from the Pacific coast.

Flimsy relocation centers were built far from the coast in valleys and far-off deserts to receive the stunned uprooted population against which, it seemed, the whole world's rage had suddenly turned. The "relocated" Japanese and Japanese Americans included persons of all ages and all occupations. Owners of urban businesses and even vast farm operations had to divest themselves of their hard-earned holdings, suddenly and under the most unfavorable of circumstances. They suffered devastating losses of personal savings and accomplishments.

Before it was all over, 110,000 Japanese Americans, including 75,000 U. S. citizens, had been forcibly moved from the west coast to detention camps. The exclusion lasted three years. They had been imprisoned without any regard for the American principal of "innocent until proven guilty."

Prior to 1942, most Americans had rested secure in the belief that the U. S. Constitution protected citizens and non-citizens equally from persecution or arrest without "due process," "weight of evidence" and "equality before the law."

I cannot forget the moment when my Santa Barbara College freshman chum, "Tack" Takahashi, called me on the telephone and in a shaky voice told me that he and his family were being sent away to a Northern California relocation camp. In the midst of this awful news, he had wished to return some books I had loaned him. The misfortune visited upon "Tack" lives in my memory as an example of the extremes to which color bias can go when people who know better remain silent.

In the days that followed the receipt of the shocking news about Tack, I spent many troubling moments attempting to reconcile the conflicting philosophies expressed by my two best college friends, Gerald Koffey and Tack, himself. Each of them intensely enjoyed my company, but Gerald's deep racial odium for anything Japanese, which he made no effort to disguise, made it impossible that we could form a close trio of comrades. Gerald habitually referred to the Japanese as "Japs," usually adding a second racist epithet. When I first noticed this severe disharmony between my friends, I naively ascribed it to a sort of jealousy between them. In matters of mutual interest, they did sometimes seem to compete for my attention. Takahashi, for his part, had simply avoided both of us when Gerald was with me.

I lost track of Tack until he looked me up one day in the early 1980s, after seeing my picture in the newspaper. He was very proud of how the Japanese Americans had rebounded after the tragedy that was visited upon them.

A Date With
The Virgin of Guadalupe

By the end of my first semester at Santa Barbara State Teacher's College, I began to realize that something ominous was casting a shadow over my life. I began to tire easily. I perspired in my sleep at night. My appetite was gone. Then, one day, as I stood before a class to give an assigned speech, I suddenly became out-of-breath and blood came out of my mouth, then I collapsed. At the time, I thought the problem was malnutrition because I had not been eating right or regularly. It turned out, however, that it was not hunger but a life-threatening lung hemorrhage. I had developed tuberculosis.

When I had to be rushed to the hospital, my teacher, Mrs. Croswell, followed me there without a moment's hesitation. Her image, grey with shock and fear, was the first I saw as I regained consciousness after having been sedated. The warmth and sympathy she radiated made me forget for a while that I was alone. I feared I might not survive until my family could arrive from Moorpark. In the eighteen months I was to be confined to the sanitarium, not one week went by that she didn't visit, always bringing me art books or equipment. She would give me assignments and share her thoughts about art.

She was a beautiful lady in her fifties. When she said to me, "Dionicio, you are my investment. You have to get well and do something with your life," I think I fell a little bit in love with her.

⌒

I shall never forget the cold horror that crept over me as I fully realized that the grim reaper who had swept away my relatives and so many of my neighbors and friends was lurking nearby.

In the 1930s, drugs for the control of TB were still unknown. The cure for TB was left almost entirely to the slow and uncertain natural powers of the body itself, aided by isolation, complete bed rest, nutrition and plenty of fruit juices. The patient lived or died, soon or gradually. Called the "rest cure," it sometimes took years. It often failed. The health department of the university had been quick to diagnose my case and immediately rushed me to the Bard Sanitarium in Ventura.

Sanitarium life in those days deprived a person of some things we never thought we could do without. Privacy, the freedom to come and go and to move about or to eat sitting up were not permitted. But sanitarium life also gave me an opportunity that few people know: To think and dream during an uninterrupted period of time. My "opportunity" lasted for almost two years. Flat on my back, I ate and did everything else that human life requires in that position. But I spent the time thinking of all the things I wanted to do for my people.

For me, those two years of forced physical inactivity allowed me to reflect on the experiences of my life and if there was to be a future. I resolved that, should I survive, I would dedicate my entire life to finding solutions for the problems that beset my fellow Mexican Americans. As I lay in bed those many months, I planned a life of usefulness to my community. That was due to a guiding light that had burst forth in my mind and kept growing brighter.

It was not that my doctors and nurses did not provide us with adequate medical assistance, but how does a youth of college age adjust to the repeated experience of having one's ward-mates die off, often suddenly, in the midst of an apparent period of improvement? How was I to adjust to the awful fact that almost everyone who came to the sanitarium died because they had come too late? But for the good fortune of having my first lung hemorrhage occur while I was in college, where proper attention was insisted upon, I might have been among those for whom it was too late.

My doctor was a man of great heart and ability... but he was a bit brusk. My first X-rays gave him little encouragement. He told me frankly, "Dionicio, in fairness to you, I must tell you that your chances to recover are not good."

Yet, my dream was just beginning. Could it be that I was not to survive to see it realized? Could it be that my life would be cut short and prevent me from ever fighting the evils which had taken such a toll on my family and numerous members of our barrio?

As for my soul, I centered my devotion on the Virgin of Guadalupe. My mother tacked her image over the head of my bed at the very beginning of my long ordeal. Her deep faith in the powers of the Virgin sustained her morale and hope. It naturally comforted me to see my mother's simple, ancient faith in action. When she left the sacred image and was about to take her leave for the day, she said, *"Hijo, ya me voy, pero ella te cuidará."* (My son, I am going now, but she will watch over you.)

When I was in elementary school, my mother had insisted that I go to Catechism classes. My father was not a devout Catholic. He would chastise me when he found out I spent an afternoon learning about saints and sins. Because of his influence, I grew up with a lukewarm view of the Church.

In stark contrast to the deep piety of my mother, was my father's extreme aversion to and contempt for what he considered hypocrisy in religion. My father recounted a personal experience from his days as a young worker in Mexico, which deepened his skepticism and anti-clerical attitudes. He said that when he worked on the demolition of an ex-convent that had been wrecked by cannon fire during the Revolution, he came across evidence of appalling skulduggery that had apparently been hidden, immured in the old building. The walls yielded many skeletons of babies, long deceased. My father had accepted the assumption, which had spread among the naive workmen, that the babies must have been the offspring of illicit relations involving the former, cloistered occupants. He accepted, without question, the further assumption that the progenitors of the infants must have been priests. In telling this story, he never mentioned any alternative explanation for the grim find.

But when my mother tacked the image of the Virgin of Guadalupe on the wall over my bed, it reinforced my sense of spiritual renewal. My mother brought centuries of Mexican heritage and faith to aid me through my illness. She would endlessly repeat that Jesus Christ, himself, sent his mother, Mary, to visit Mexico soon after the Spanish Conquest. The Virgin Mary, she said, had appeared in person to an Indian shepherd, Juan Diego, on a hill called Tepeyac. The Virgin had brought a message of special heavenly affection for all Mexicans. Since few would believe an Indian shepherd, she emblazoned her dark image on his cloak, which is preserved to this day in the new Basilica of Guadalupe on the outskirts of Mexico City. The Virgin of Guadalupe's appearance as a dark-faced "Mother of God" to a humble Indian was widely accepted as a symbol of heaven's special protection for the natives of Mexico and the Americas.

After my phrenesectomy (lung operation), I was much encouraged by various signs of recovery. The long days, weeks and months of complete bed rest were not without some relief. I became spokesman for the patients and editor of the patient's mimeographed newspaper, "The Bard Interview." I even took a college course, "Business English," right there in my bed. A teacher was provided for me. I continued to draw. A special easel was designed so that I could charcoal-draw lying on my back. I became a minor authority on the prevention of the spread of tuberculosis and wrote articles on it for the instruction of my fellow inmates. Later, my research on this subject was to pay off as I produced a term paper in college on the subject, which earned me an "A" in a public health course.

There were some frustrating negative elements in my environment. One was a doctor who seemed to be skilled enough technically, but whose philosophy about T.B. and heredity irritated me no end. I would not have been surprised if an uninstructed layman visiting our largely "Spanish-speaking" ill population would have thought that there was a connection between Mexican heritage and T.B. But this doctor, who should have been more knowledgeable, declared, "Mexicans are especially susceptible by biological makeup to T.B." This doctor had never visited the barrios in which our people existed, he had never been to Walnut Canyon, he had never seen us up at dawn and at work in the orchards when we were six years old. He did not realize that we became "men" at ten and were expected to assume the back-breaking activities of pickers.

On the lighter side, it was satisfying to have the company of so many beautiful Mexican American girls as fellow patients in that sanitarium. But it was depressing to reflect on their presence in that scene of constant tragedy. I often heard their names in the conversations of nurses chatting about patients who had recently suffered a pulmonary hemorrhage and died. "Last night, Guadalupe died." "Last night, Manuela hemorrhaged, and she died this morning." "Dr. So and So says María will be lucky to live through the week!"

I had remained determined to give the best fight within my power for survival and for the opportunity to combat the evils which had become so real to me through personal experience. I would let nothing stand in the way. My recovery took eighteen long months. The doctor demanded that I eliminate every single unnecessary physical movement. Even my breathing, he said, should be consciously governed and modulated. My determination to survive never faltered, and from one X-ray to the next I concentrated all my willpower on the elimination of the tell-tale shadows on those plates.

When eighteen months had passed, my doctor came to my bedside and said, "Okay, stand up!" They were beautiful words, but in the literal sense, I knew he was teasing. One loses the capacity to walk in eighteen months. It took me five months to relearn to perform most of life's vital functions, including how to urinate standing up. I never wanted to see a hospital bed pan or a urinal ever again. I had to readjust to being in an upright position and viewing the environment from a normal, but long unaccustomed perspective. How wonderfully strange it seemed to shave and bathe and even to eat in a standing or sitting position!

But my rebirth was all glorious sunshine! I knew I had won a bout with death. I was grateful to the Virgin of Guadalupe and to all those who helped me see my world again and start putting together the pieces of my dream. The reassurance that my successful phrenesectomy brought me, inspired an exhilarating feeling of success. Not just the success of the moment, but the promise of accomplishment in the life that was now more likely to be.

In the eighteen months I had lain on my back, as I recall, I never let despondency fully control me. Perhaps the key was the absorbing activity program with which I filled my waking hours. I had eighteen bedridden months to fill and I did it! I involved my mind and my creativity in order to do it. I could not rely on outside stimuli to fill the endless hours. I kept busy in every way possible. What a joy to learn to finger paint in bed! It was so easy and relaxing. How I enjoyed creating art to give to my fellow patients. My eight-year-old brother, Tim, used to bring me butterflies which I would arrange in countless patterns. Then, I would examine the iridescent beauty of the wings of these gorgeous, delicate little creatures. Somehow I had never fully appreciated them before. They symbolized the beauty of life for me.

When I relearned to walk and get around, at long last, after almost two years, I took my leave of my hopeful companions and went home.

An Exile in my own Barrio

Home! After almost two years! I foresaw the excitement of a traditional Mexican fiesta welcoming me. I anticipated the joyful gathering of all my dear old neighbors and friends—the smiling faces, the *abrazos*, the music, the aroma of a welcoming barrio fiesta! But it was not to be. My neighbors and friends had a mortal terror of the infirmity I had suffered. The awful truth soon became apparent to me: Among my own neighbors I was shunned as a pariah at the very moment of the greatest triumph of my life! In subsequent days of reflection, I realized that my neighbors and friends were completely innocent of any understanding of the meaning of an "arrested infection," the closest thing to a "cure" for tuberculosis known to medicine in the 1930s.

And my family! They saved the day for me and my memories of it forever! Our tradition prescribed a joyful, colorful, musical fiesta. As my father drove me up to the house in the Model T, bright tissue-paper decorations greeted me. My mother, who was the finest cook in the whole area, outdid herself. Her fiesta banquet had everything—chicken in *mole* sauce, barbecued pig and all the delectable trimmings of a "banquet fit for a king" in the rich Tarascan tradition. She was convinced that I had not had a decent meal in eighteen months.

I had envisioned that my welcome home would be reminiscent of the community jamborees with which my grandfather and family had been received ten years before. Well, the neighbors weren't there, but twenty-one members of my family were—it was a twenty-one person salute. I felt like king for a day. But what was just as heartwarming was my dog's excitement. He ran from one end of the lot to the other, barking his own welcome.

As I stepped out of the Model T with my cane, I saw my mother crying under the walnut tree. As she smiled at me, I saw her tears of happiness. She was not one to run down and embrace me. She was too reticent. The intensity of her quiet emotion overwhelmed me. She had put on her best dress for the occasion, the pink one with the polka dots, and a freshly starched bonnet. She had a dark grey *rebozo* (shawl) over her shoulders. To be home again with my mother, more beautiful than the *Mona Lisa*, was the reawakening of all the resolve to accomplish those things I had planned during my illness. I remember going up to her and putting my arm around her. I said, "Mother, thank you. Because of your faith, I am here today."

A Spark Ignites a Cause

During the interlude while I was once again in Moorpark, before returning to college, I was troubled once again by segregation in the theater. I decided once and for all that I would do something about it.

It was 1940, four years after Margaret Mitchell's "Gone With the Wind" was published, and I, along with millions of Americans, had waited with great anticipation to see the spectacular epic that David O. Selznick had created from one of the most popular novels in the United States at that time.

On the night the film opened in our little country movie house, I had carefully prepared to take advantage of the opportunity to move forward with my plan of action. My school girlfriend and I were involved in the scheme. It is said that there are many moments in a person's life that stand out relentlessly against any background of acute pain and tragedy. The tragedy of what occurred that evening is still vivid in my mind. It had nothing to do with Rhett Butler's obsession with the spoiled and flirtatious Scarlett O'Hara who spurned his love. But it had everything to do with me personally.

After purchasing our tickets, an usher showed us to our seats, which were in the right-hand section traditionally reserved for Mexicans. My friend and I ignored her and picked out our own seats in the middle section, something I had thoroughly discussed with my friend. I had become fed up with the way I had always been treated. I was inwardly fuming and the flames became more intense with this whole concept of Mexicans being segregated in a movie house because they were not deemed good enough to sit next to

Anglos. "You Mexicans smell," they would exclaim. "You don't take baths and you smell like garlic."

Shocked at my impudence and with what she considered a crisis on her hands, the usher rushed to the rear of the theater for help. She returned with a husky man, a former classmate of mine, who had taken our tickets. They both insisted that we move to the Mexican section. I was outraged. The test that I had planned to put into play wasn't working, but I felt it was too late to give in. When I declined to move, the former school mate grabbed me by my arm and yanked me from my seat.

That enraged me more, and I felt a blistering and unprecedented urge to kill. Suddenly, the screen went dark, the lights came on and the entire audience turned to watch the drama playing out before its eyes. Even my friends in the audience seemed annoyed that I was creating a disturbance, many of them only dimly aware of the real significance of the incident they were witnessing. They didn't care. They joined the others in shouting for us to sit down. Finally, my partner in the protest abandoned me, leaving her seat to sit with her friends. Seconds later, I was hustled out of the theater and my 25 cents was refunded.

I found myself expelled from the theater, with nothing to do but to walk home, alone. My rage, however, had not subsided. I imagined all sorts of scenes. I could still hear the shrill and contemptuous voices shouting vulgarities at me as my former schoolmate attempted to put me in my place. "Don't you know where you belong? Don't ever try that again."

The shame I felt was for all my people who were constantly being treated in this humiliating manner. There was no doubt in my mind that it was they, the so-called privileged, who were cruel, short-sighted and uncivilized. But it did not make me feel any better because, after all, they held all the cards. At that moment, I felt as if that woman who had expelled me from the theater with her racist slurs had looked down on me, even though I was much taller. I couldn't help thinking about my father's repeated warnings to stay away from *"ese teatro mugroso"* (that filthy theater), which dared to humiliate our people. But that was the only entertainment we looked forward to, especially the Saturday afternoon matinees.

Only a person who has been physically seized, pushed and shoved under such circumstances and at such a youthful age can understand the rage I felt. I was not alone in my feelings. This event was to cause quite a stir among my own people. After all, it concerned a shy, mild mannered young man, who was a good student, not a troublemaker. But more importantly, the target of discrimination was the son of Severo Morales, who was now one of the two most successful Mexican businessmen in Moorpark. My father had already come to his own conclusion about how offensive the theater's policy was. His feelings were so strong that my brother, Trinidad, and I would have to sneak out of the house on Saturday mornings, when we were younger, to go to that theater. When he asked us where we had been, we would lie and say we had been to a friend's house. Those were the days when we didn't know any better.

Severo Morales was a man to be reckoned with. Due to his status, he always had an audience and he was the theater's worst enemy. His derogatory criticisms never ended. He was forever insisting on a boycott. Of course, that never happened. What else was there to do for entertainment in our tiny town?

The indignity of how I had been treated was more than I could bear. It hurt even more because this degradation had been inflicted by a young man who had been my classmate and teammate. I had played marbles with him! We had, quite literally, grown up together and, I thought, had never before looked upon each other as being "different." Now, suddenly, he had put his hands on me. He had grabbed my arm and violently shoved me, publicly insulting me before an audience of my neighbors and friends. I walked home and, as I sat on our front steps, I was momentarily seized by depression and self-pity. To this day, his actions are as incomprehensible to me as they were on that day, more than fifty years ago.

That particular episode was the first time I fought back, and I lost. I was determined to find another way and it was this profound anger seething within me that became the basis for what I was to do next.

It was "them" against "us." My mind was set for action. I would find a way.

Doing Something About It!

During the next few weeks, hardly an hour passed when I did not ask myself, "What can be done to remedy this hateful policy of our movie house?" I spent many sleepless nights plotting. I would spend evenings talking to my mother about my longing for the day when I could sit wherever I wanted to in a public movie house. It didn't seem like much to ask. Yet, I had never seen a theater in Southern California, except in Los Angeles itself, where the policy of segregating our people did not prevail. I resented hearing the words from the mouths of ushers, indicating bruskly where I belonged. Often, when I would accompany visiting college friends from Santa Barbara to our movie house, I would face the same damnable treatment, which knocked my self-esteem out of the ballpark.

When my mother fully realized the intensity with which I was determined to sit where I wanted to at the movies, she suggested I talk to Don Lucas Pérez. My mother's timely advice would turn out to be the key to the history-making solution we were striving for. Don Lucas was a humble man of great wisdom. He was also a talented orator with a philosophical turn of mind. It was to him our people turned as the organizer of our community's major cultural and patriotic events, such as the celebrations of the Cinco de Mayo and the Mexican Independence Day.

Fortunately for us, as we prepared to move on the matter of the segregated theater, Don Lucas had long been recognized by the Mexican Consulate General in Los Angeles as leader of our community and *presidente* of our local *Honorífica Mexicana*. The *Honorífica* was the most important cultural, protective and cooperative association in our little corner of the world, Walnut Canyon.

When I talked with Don Lucas, he surprised me by also revealing his own deep anger at the way the local theater was run. He seemed filled with the same bitter resentment at the maltreatment of our people at the Moorpark movie house that had so stirred my father's anger. He startled me during our interview by drawing up what amounted to a battle plan. I was pleased that we agreed that immediate action was called for. He said that since the demands of struggle we were about to undertake were beyond the resources of our local community, he would go personally to seek the guidance and active assistance of the Mexican Consul General in Los Angeles.

Don Lucas brought back to Walnut Canyon the good news that we had the solid support of the law on our side. California law, we were informed, specifically prohibited the segregation of anyone on the basis of race or national origin in any place of public accommodation within the state. This law was not without teeth. There was a fine of $50 per person, per offense, payable to the victim of segregation, personally. The minimum $50 fine assessed in the 1940s would compare to a $500 penalty today. Now we knew we were on the right track, at last!

Through Don Lucas, the attorneys of the Consulate's Department of Protection gave us the green light to move ahead confidently. We immediately began to put together the first Mexican mass meeting in the history of Simi Valley.

When the historic evening arrived, we gathered in the public hall of the local Four Square Hall. The consul's attorneys opened the proceedings by explaining the legal rights involved by assuring us that everyone in our town who had been discriminated against had a cause of legal action under the state law. As the stirring oratory from the podium increased, the crowd's excitement rose to a climax.

In the meantime, the message had somehow already reached the manager of the El Rancho movie house. She already knew about the action we were "secretly conspiring" to take. Just as we were about to adjourn, there was a sudden stir in the audience. An important-looking Anglo, who was a total stranger to us, entered the hall and asked permission to speak to us. With calm assurance he announced that the segregation policies of the El Rancho had been abolished that very day by order of the management. He concluded by inviting the meeting to send a delegation to the theater to check on the authenticity of his history-making announcement.

Don Lucas' son, Luis and I, made up the committee. We went to the theater, bought our tickets and were allowed to sit anywhere we chose. The great weight of years of helpless compliance with a bad custom was suddenly and forever lifted from my heart.

There were applause and cheers from the expectant crowd when we returned and delivered the message we had longed to hear. WE HAD WON!

Insights from Steinbeck

The doctors, at long last, had given me my final release to return to school. While I had been in the sanitarium, I had read all of John Steinbeck's writings. He broadened my perspective on the problems of hunger, poverty and desperation. Steinbeck, in his *Grapes of Wrath*, articulated eloquently many of the same ideas I was beginning to form about the human condition. He opened my eyes and gave me a framework for understanding the plight of our people. His writings taught me the invaluable lesson that human misery was not the exclusive plight of any particular people.

Steinbeck often wrote about Mexicans in Monterey County during the depression years. In his books, I began to discover the historical roots of our own Mexican American life, in our same setting, only in an earlier period of California history. I was transported by his descriptions of our people. He inspired me to seek the broader picture.

No public school class had ever taught me that California had already been organized as a state under a Mexican governor—a state with a rich spiritual and temporal culture as well as a prosperous agricultural economy. All of this, of course, was before the coming of the "pioneers" and gold-seekers from the East.

I read other authors and became enthralled by the political courage and foresight of the Mexican *Californio* leadership. I imagined myself sitting as a spectator in Colton Hall in Monterey, witnessing the proceedings of the Constitutional Convention of 1849. I envisioned a delegation of eight distinguished *Californios*, who had been prominent under the Mexican regime, as they created history. These brave men stood their ground and spoke their minds, both in

English and Spanish, hoping to give our state a good start in
its new life. We have only to look around us to note that the
names of these Mexican American constitutional fathers.
They live on in the names of the boulevards and cities of
modern California.

There was José Antonio Carrillo, who had signed
Mexico's first constitution, which had abolished slavery four
decades before Abraham Lincoln signed the Emancipation
Proclamation. There were General Mariano Vallejo, Pablo de
la Guerra and José Covarrubias of Santa Barbara; Miguel de
Pedrorena, whom Commodore Stockton had appointed
Customs Collector at San Diego; Antonio Pico, the popular
mayor of San Jose; Jacinto Rodríguez, a militiaman from
Monterey and San Francisco; wealthy landowner and rancher Manuel Domínguez of Los Angeles (described as a
dark-complexioned mestizo and even as the "Indian member" of the Convention.) What a preview of things to come!
They fought for the rights of all California inhabitants to
become citizens, regardless of race, a concept not accepted
in the rest of the United States.

The presence of Domínguez among the drafters of the
state constitution had a considerable impact on the convention, particularly when it came time to debate an Anglo
delegate's proposition that, "voting in California should be
limited to white males only." Had I been a voting member of
that delegation, as dark-complexioned as I am, I would probably have felt like an outcast. Santa Barbara's delegate,
Pablo de la Guerra, led the argument against the "white
males only" policy. He pointed out that the Treaty of
Guadalupe Hidalgo, which ended the war with Mexico, had
guaranteed the former Mexican citizens American citizenship and the right to vote under the new regime, without
any color discrimination. The "white only" proposition, of
course, opposed the dark-complexioned delegate

Domínguez's right to sign the very constitution he was helping to draft.

What a lesson for us in the twentieth century. The
racists of our own day should know that while bias in
California has existed from the very beginning, it was also
vigorously opposed from the beginning by Mexican leaders!

When I was in high school history classes, the 49ers
and their Gold Rush had always been glamorized and
romanticized. No teacher ever mentioned to me that the discovery of gold at Sutter's Mill attracted thousands of "gold
crazy" Yankees to California, many of whom were hysterical,
mob-minded and lynch-minded. Now, I read how they quickly extinguished the human and property rights of the
Californios. They even went to the extent of expelling them
from the gold-bearing areas, despite their rights of ownership. The falsely glamorized "Gold Rush" was, in actuality,
for "white Yankees only." Many prudent Californios abandoned their hope of finding gold and returned to their
homes and ranches, to their trades and firesides, to be safe
from the "vigilante" excesses of the gold-crazed mobs. And
to think, Mexicans had discovered and mined gold before
the Yankee "discovery" and fever ever existed. And just as
important, Mexicans had discovered mercury in California,
which made the mining possible.

That the former Mexican, newly "Mexican American"
Californios were to quickly become "foreigners in their own
land" became clear, even on the floor of the constitutional
convention at Colton Hall in Monterey. On at least one occasion, white southerners, including delegate William Gwin,
formerly of Tennessee, had the nerve to call delegate
Carrillo, who had been involved in California affairs for thirty years, a "foreigner." He got a good tongue lashing from
Carrillo in reply. Humble, silent submission to personal
abuse was just not the Carrillo family's way. He was coura-

geous and forthright, and not about to take personal abuse even from the "conqueror."

In the 1850s, there seemed a glimmer of hope for a rational, multi-ethnic California society, living in peace and conciliation. But by the 1880's, the Californios found themselves reduced to second-class citizenship.

As I absorbed the facts of California's unromanticized beginnings, I was reminded of the parallels to conditions that still exist today! We are engaged in a struggle to protect our rights, and that struggle has deep roots in the history of the Southwest.

Undercover Among Braceros

The large first wave of *bracero* farm workers arrived in the United States during World War II while I was still a student at Santa Barbara State Teacher's College. I soon became increasingly incensed about the constant reports of abuses of the rights of these farm workers. Between classes, I became involved in community activities from Moorpark to Santa Barbara. It occurred to me that the *Bracero* Program might be a good test of my skills. Somehow, even without special preparation, I passed the Civil Service Examination, and the following month went to work for the Department of Agriculture.

Just as I was about to start my new job, the tragic news came of my brother Trinidad's death. The tentacles of tuberculosis had reached our family again, for the fifth time. Trini was only twenty-one years old. Editor of the Moorpark Union High School student newspaper, he had won many medals in oratory and debate. At the time of his death, he was awaiting his final interview for acceptance to Stanford University. I still carry the scar of that personal tragedy and the near decimation of our family. I was saddened by my brother's death, but still reported for work. My duties were those of a federal compliance officer for the War Food Administration of the Department of Agriculture.

The *Bracero* Program was the result of an international agreement set up to legally import farm labor from Mexico. The shortage of manpower in the United States during the war had become acute. The powerful California growers had used their influence in Congress to pass legislation for the importation of field workers from Mexico. Agribusiness needed people from Mexico in wartime and no politician dared offer any opposition. The growers testified they were going broke. Mexican Americans had joined the Army and there was no one to pick the crops.

The *Bracero* Program turned out to be a grand opportunity for the growers to assume almost absolute control over their laborers. They housed them, fed them and created a fear of possible deportation if the workers got out of line. I was one of the officers who had the authority to repatriate them. Actually, even the offense of not producing as much as a fellow worker was deemed sufficient to earn the involuntary "quick trip" south. But no matter what my personal sentiments, the workers were perceived as virtually belonging to the growers. Here, they were wage slaves or peons in the middle of the twentieth century in the "land of the free!"

Between 1941 and 1946, and again between 1951 and 1957, giant agribusiness growers in the Rio Grande Valley of Texas and the San Joaquin Valley of California maintained their multimillionaire status at the expense of Mexican labor. It became fashionable, in fact, for the typical son or daughter of a grower to brag to friends as to how many *braceros* the family controlled.

But what really angered me was the fact that many growers were not in compliance with the rules of the *Bracero* Program. On top of it all, not only the growers, but local police officials, too, had gotten into the act. In many small towns, the police would pick up any *bracero* out late on pay night. His fine in court would be, coincidentally, just the amount the man had on him. The usual charge would be "drunkenness in public." Local exploiters also got into the *bracero*-feeding racket and the prostitution business. In some towns, the chiefs of police would supply the camps with both the feeding kitchens and the illicit trade in women. Other opportunists made a habit of visiting the camps with truckloads of shoddy merchandise for sale at exorbitant prices. I noticed that some of our own Mexican American people got onto the gravy train themselves. Some actually became pawns for the growers, further exploiting the farm workers. Overnight, some of them actually became wealthy, too. Thus, began the first chapter of my experiences with the *Bracero* Program.

I do not hesitate to commend the growers who complied with the International Labor Agreement. But they too proved again that there is a cycle of when Mexican labor is needed and when it is not.

When the program ended, I still wanted to find a job that would further my mission in life. I didn't want to deviate from my goal. I piddled around for a few months with a job in the Los Angeles County Probation Office, in the Delinquency Prevention Division. I was assigned to the Alpine, Loma and Palo Verde gangs. Supposedly, the whole responsibility was to get gangs involved in sports and social activities which would steer them away from crime. Despite all the genuine efforts made to attack the problem, the program never quite got off the ground. It had been set up just after the Sleepy Lagoon murder case involving *pachuco* gangs had been resolved. None of the higher-ups knew how to handle this perplexing problem of youth delinquency and they failed to provide adequate guidance. Juvenile delinquency was just as monumentally difficult to address then as it is today.

The only deputy probation officers who remained on the job were those who passed the County Civil Service Examination, but they didn't know beans about handling these supposedly hard-to-reach youngsters. Even back in those days, press coverage of gang fights glamorized gangs and gave them self-esteem when they saw their names in print. Gangs offered too much comfort, prestige and security to barrio youth who often only found rejection in school and in society's other institutions.

I had many conversations with Manny Villalobos, a brilliant, tall, good-looking seventeen-year-old who was the leader of the Alpine gang. He would often say to me, "The only thing I got that gives me muscle and respect is having the guys look up to me. Nothing else is important."

After a few months of working with gangs, my interest in the official and accepted remedies subsided. Gang activity outlasted the short-lived program. That was the summer of 1945.

The colorful attire of the zoot suited gang members, however, made a long-lasting impression on me. Neat, immaculate dress with brightly shined shoes, well pressed suits and broad-brimmed hats remain for me the symbols of that unforgettable generation.

San Antonio Sojourn

After my brief East L.A. experience, I returned to Moorpark to be with my father, who was in failing health. I helped out in the store as he suffered one stroke after another. After he died in 1949, I felt that I needed to pursue my cause and apply my ideas for barrio organization and community action in other areas. I had heard there was an opening in a barrio service organization in San Antonio. Henry Gonzales, later to serve as a U.S. Congressman, had just resigned the directorship of the Pan American Progressive Association. It was a job that seemed made-to-order for me. I flew to Texas, was interviewed and accepted for the post.

San Antonio means a lot to Texans. They call it "The Gateway to the Americas." In the very heart of the city stands the Alamo, the dual symbol of the labors of the mission padres and of the later clash of cultures in the days of Generals Santa Anna and Sam Houston. To Mexican Americans, San Antonio is particularly meaningful, for it includes one of the largest urban colonies of Mexicans and Mexican Americans in the nation. But when I arrived, I had difficulty understanding why most of our people preferred to be called "Latin Americans." The Anglos, on the other hand, simply referred to us as "Messkins."

I had always been fascinated with San Antonio. My young wife, María, who was born in San Antonio, heightened my interest in the colorful Texas city. She was convinced that things were so miserable in that Texas urban colony that someone needed to go there and continue the work of Henry Gonzales.

At a convention, I heard a ringing address by Archbishop Robert E. Lucey, who deplored the substandard conditions of the poor in San Antonio's Mexican American communities. He spoke of the frightful health and sanitary conditions in *las colonias* and depicted the political powerlessness and hopelessness of our people there. He eloquently described the grinding poverty and hunger, particularly, as it affected children.

Archbishop Lucey was a native of Los Angeles. When I first met him, as Monsignor Lucey, he had already become a hero to our people for extending Catholic social services to the long neglected Mexican population of Los Angeles. He succeeded, against powerful anti-Mexican feeling, even among the Catholics, because of the valiant support of Los Angeles' Bishop (later Archbishop) John J. Cantwell.

I was fortunate to have had the opportunity to experience San Antonio as a prelude to my anticipated career in East Los Angeles. I committed myself to one year there. I picked up and moved to San Antonio. My wife and baby girl, Margarita, followed me three months later.

I was a total newcomer to the area. I knew no one. Archbishop Lucey suggested that one of the first persons of the many I would see should be Dr. Héctor García, who was founder of the American G. I. Forum, an important civil rights organization.

Although Dr. García was a native of Corpus Christi, when he came to San Antonio, he did me the honor of swearing me into membership in the San Antonio Chapter of the Forum. Never did I leave his presence without a renewed impulse to battle against the nearly impossible plight of our people in San Antonio.

I was soon to meet attorney Gus Garcia, a colorful pioneer activist, who was one of the finest orators I had ever met.

I was much encouraged when attorney Alonzo Perales, one of the founders of the League of United Latin American Citizens (LULAC), the other great civil rights organization, allowed me to become his disciple during my year in San Antonio. Sick at heart, I addressed him, "I am stunned and shaken at the venomous bigotry that pervades this American city." He said that racism in Texas was even more intense in rural towns and smaller cities, from one side of the state to the other.

My first face-to-face experience with the misery of San Antonio's barrios can only be described as deeply traumatic. Everything the archbishop had decried turned out to be true. His words had hardly done justice to the appalling inhumanity of conditions existing in the Alamo City. I simply found it impossible to believe that what I saw, heard and smelled was real. Could it be that a great modern city, under the American flag, in the proud State of Texas, would permit it's Mexican Americans to live and die in such miserable poverty and inhumane living conditions? The year was 1950.

Sometimes I imagined for fleeting moments that I was in India... perhaps in Calcutta or in the favela of some poverty-stricken city in Brazil. The infant mortality rate was incredibly high; diarrhea was almost universal and tuberculosis raged through the ranks of the aged and the young, unchecked—even unrecognized. Even in those smogless days, the atmosphere in *las colonias* reeked with the nauseating stench of over-full outhouses and tons of uncollected trash. Aging garbage rotted in the sweltering sun on every street and vacant lot.

Las colonias was one place where a person with his eyes shut could guide himself from one place to another merely by his sense of smell. Even the drinking water stank and tasted bad. It was not delivered through underground pipes from clean sources. In *las colonias* it was delivered by cart. Ancient, hundred-gallon tanks were horse-drawn through the hot streets to fill the oil-drum storage tanks of the various families at thirty-five cents a load. From what I saw, many of the rusty tanks and the drums were lined with algae. The water was always lukewarm, with a repulsive, metallic flavor. I know this because as I walked through the area, I got so thirsty, I had to drink the water. Water was so costly and scarce among the unemployed and poor that it was almost never put out in pans for the dogs. It was a common sight to watch dehydrated pets stagger from house to house with their frothy tongues hanging out in a desperate life-or-death hunt for the life-sustaining liquid. I often wondered how, under such circumstances, anyone could get together enough clean water for a decent bath. I don't know how they did it, but most people managed to sustain their cleanliness.

During my short span of involvement with community work in San Antonio, checking on discrimination was a major assignment. One of my first assignments was to investigate discrimination at local swimming pools. I chose to bring to a popular, local swimming pool a young, light-skinned and light-haired, undocumented immigrant who had recently crossed the border at El Paso. He stood in line in front of me and paid for his ticket, no questions were asked and not a word of English was spoken. I then handed my twenty-five cents to the cashier. She responded, "Can't you read? No Mexicans are allowed here." I said to her, "I am an American citizen. The person you just sold a ticket to is the *real* Mexican."

A desperate effort was made to find this young Mexican who had slipped in because he was of lighter complexion. They never found him. I was ecstatic about that. I waited for Mario and we went to the nearest bar and celebrated. Although the incident had underlying sad elements of the discrimination that existed then, we laughed because we'd pulled off our experiment and proved our point about racism.

⌐━━

Most of the time *las colonias* had a half-dead look, for most of the working people had to board up their houses during harvest time and leave their homes for such distant places as northern California and Michigan. They traveled in their old pickups or huddled in large, outdated trucks. They all knew that joining the migrant labor stream was the only way to survive.

Into this depressing situation I came. I could see that the rest of the community and the rest of the nation needed to be awakened to the atrocities which our people were suffering in San Antonio. I had no resources, not even a car. I had to walk everywhere.

In those early days, it seemed to me that organization and direct political action were needed. I became Executive Director of the Pan American Progressive Association at a salary of $25 a week. On this meager wage, I started my little family ever perilously close to economic disaster. But, this was what I wanted to do.

There was no federal or state funding of such action groups then. The barrio residents and Mexican business leaders themselves had to try to raise our little budget by personal contributions. My assignment made me, for the first time, a paid political advocate, full time. I served as a professional ombudsman in *las colonias.*

Las colonias were organized and mapped into 21 neighborhood subdivisions, each represented by a committee and a local chairman. I would meet with them to coordinate their efforts to bring community problems and needs to official municipal attention. The year went fast. But walking the streets of San Antonio was for me a veritable university of barrio problem-solving. Since I saw no expectations of an increase in salary or better strategies for attacking the local problems, I did not renew my contract. We all decided it was best that we return to Los Angeles.

Braceros Again

Back home again, I found out the *Bracero* Program had been revived. Congress had once again found the nation to be in need of Mexican labor—as before, the growers had testified they were in trouble. This time, I found a position in the Department of Labor. On my first day of duty this second time around, I was hit by a double-barreled problem: The boss was ill. His assistant was on vacation. His secretary called in that she would be late, very late. At about five minutes after eight, the bookkeeper came in and handed me a heavy federal employee's manual to study up on federal procedures. At about 8:15, a frantic call came in from the regional office at San Francisco that 500 workers had gone out on strike in our region. "We" (who turned out to be me) were expected to settle it and report back immediately.

Fortunately, I had some labor mediating experience in my previous work with lemon pickers. I borrowed the most impressive car in the motor pool, one with the federal insignia emblazoned on the doors. I also borrowed a briefcase from my supervisor. It was embossed with the gold federal eagle. When I got to the camp where the strikers were waiting, they were amazed and pleased to see me, an official of Mexican descent who could speak Spanish. They actually applauded. We reached a settlement without difficulty when an examination of the facts revealed that the workers were being paid less than the prevailing wage. Problem resolved!

I wish that I could report that all our problems were that easy, or that my personal job safety was entirely secure as I proceeded to delve deeper into actual cases of grower violations of the terms of the international labor agreement.

What made my investigative work all the more adventurous this time were the unusual methods that I devised in the line of my official duties. They were considered unorthodox both by my co-workers and my bosses. I had discovered an unprecedented investigative tool. I built upon my Tarascan physical features by wearing clothes, on occasion, like those of a field worker. Even this disguise, which I used to identify myself with my *bracero* friends, offered me the new experience of completely changing my appearance and successfully melting into the crowd of workers.

On appropriate occasions I would change my attire completely. I would put on a large maroon plaid and quilted jacket with a brick-red shirt, buttoned to the collar underneath. I wore work weary unwashed denims and weather-beaten field work shoes of unfinished leather, splattered with mud. I topped this all off with a straw hat from Michoacan, a *Saguayo*, with the typical colorful tassel hanging from the back. I had engineered my own "private eye" outfit. I even had a special pocket sewn into my jacket to conceal a small tape recorder. So equipped, I had no need to use a notebook, as my Anglo fellow agents did. Of course, it was impossible for them to lose themselves in the *bracero* crowds. And their notebooks did scare the simple country farm workers, who were much more at ease giving me the real facts, with no intimidating outward signs from me of sleuthing or note taking.

My charge was to investigate complaints lodged with the Mexican consulate. Of course, my main advantage was that although I was visually indistinguishable from my *bracero* friends, they still knew who I was. Of course, some of my fellow agents resented my investigative techniques, which they loudly denounced as unethical. That never bothered me in the least.

I always reported to my office at eight o'clock in the morning in a white shirt, tie and three-piece suit. Later, when I sensed it to be necessary, I would change my disguise.

Among my many investigative chores came a report that prostitution was being openly exploited in a certain Northern California camp, a clear violation of the international agreement. The women were being brought in from Tijuana. The fees charged were $15.00 with a five dollar cut for the foreman; so ran the report.

Getting the evidence was another matter and arriving at the scene undiscovered was an even greater challenge. So I decided to walk to the camp, after the evening movie, along with some braceros from the local town, three miles away. Among the countless facts I uncovered that evening, it became clear that the camp manager had been conducting business as a procurer on the side. I had caught him red-handed.

On another occasion, I learned that a company truck driver, whose job was to transport the laborers to work, was an alcoholic. He would drive his bus recklessly, in a drunken condition, to the horror of his passengers. I got up early one day and, in my disguise, took the ride to work with this driver who hauled the workers to a lemon grove. I suffered the same terror of which his regular passengers had complained. I confronted the driver, showed him my federal badge and notified the local authorities. The driver was immediately discharged.

On the pleasant side, I recall the fond memory of how I enjoyed many evenings in those days, around campfires or in the bunkhouses with the workers. I listened to stories of their families, so far away, and of the sacrifice and deprivation they had experienced. They always reminisced about the beauties of Mexico: "*Mexico, lindo y querido.*"

Many of them had been obliged to sell their chickens, goats, saddles, even their family cows and horses to raise the money for the *mordida* (bribe) that had to be paid to mayors in Mexico who were in charge of recruiting the prospective workers in their home villages. These corrupt officials would not issue the required U. S. contract applications without a substantial payment. Unfortunately for those field laborers, so anxious to work north of the border, they would have to deal with the entrenched and crooked local officials.

One time, disguised as a *bracero*, I waited in line for a regular meal being served at a certain camp. Of course, they did not notice me and filled my plate with pork striplings disguised with plenty of red chile. They called it *chile colorado*. I took my plate to be analyzed by the Nutrition Department at Santa Barbara College. It turned out to be 87% fat and unfit for human consumption. I am happy to say we were able to shut down that camp.

During the *bracero* years, substandard housing continued to be a problem. But not all growers were guilty of non-compliance. Gradually, reform began and the better employers built decent living facilities. Growers at Oxnard, Santa Barbara and Santa Maria, to name only a few, often maintained standards above the requirements of Public Law 78 in matters of food and housing.

Transportation and on-the-job accidents were a problem. There were seventy-nine fatal accidents in 1957 alone. Machinery unfamiliar to the braceros (tractors, choppers, etc.) caused many injuries and deaths, as did rickety trucks used to transport as many as fifty workers at a time. Neglected brakes failed, trucks fell into canals and some were hit by trains. I was involved in the investigation of some of these tragedies.

Industrial poisons also hurt many braceros. Pesticide spraying from the air was done while braceros were in the fields beneath. Reportedly, one poor worker even had his head chopped off by a low-flying plane.

In later years, great improvements were made in the treatment and safety of all farm workers under the leadership of my friend, César Chávez and the United Farm Workers Union that he pioneered. I met this father of unionization of farm workers in my early years of working with the braceros. We'd have vehement discussions in those early days, and I began to understand and admire his philosophy of peaceful liberation when he was first involved with the East Los Angeles Community Organization in the early 50s. We had many things in common, including the fact that we had both been born in Yuma.

But the whole *Bracero* Program had been sort of pushed on Mexico. The people at the top couldn't care less about the well-being of workers. Perhaps, many were not fully aware of the level of exploitation. The authorities in Mexico were perhaps unaware, too, that one Mexican was being pitted against another as imported workers competed against domestic Mexican American labor.

One day, the news reached me that my mother's cousin, Ana, had run off with a *bracero* from Oaxaca. He had been under my jurisdiction. When he took Ana with him to Mexico, his contract had terminated. Ironically, I had been the one who had introduced them in the first place. The young man's name was Apolello Rosas. Soon after the elopement, the *Bracero* Program came to an end and I forgot all about Apolello and Ana's romantic interlude.

Years later, in 1975, on one of my trips to Oaxaca, the local papers ran stories about my arrival as guest of the Mexican Federal Department of Indigenous Education, as a visitor from California to the Oaxaca Cultural Institute.

During that visit, a note was thrust into my hand by a total stranger. The note was from Apolello Rosas. It read, "Ana is very sick. Can you please come? She knows you are in Oaxaca and has been asking for you. Apolello" I was surprised, concerned and deeply moved.

The following day, I was taken by a state official to the village of San Pedro de Galilea. When I arrived, Mr. Rosas recognized me and quickly led me to Ana. She greeted me standing in front of her little thatched hut, decked out in her best Zapotecan embroidered blouse. She was still attractive, but I noted the dark rings under her eyes and her alarming pallor. Suddenly, I realized I was looking at the very image of my mother. They could have been twins. The resemblance was incredible.

When I asked what was being done for her, Apolello replied that she was in the care of one of the most admired *curanderas* in Oaxaca. I was to discover that Ana was suffering a raging fever and great weakness. No one could tell me what her illness was. I invited her to return with me to the United States, where she could receive modern medical attention, for she was herself a U. S. citizen. Apolello would not hear of such a thing. He told me "I would die here alone and would never see her again. I would rather remain by her side during her illness." Apolello then turned to his wife and spoke quietly to her in Zapotec. From his tone of voice I could sense that his decision was final.

It was time for me to leave. I handed them all the loose dollars I had in my possession, which Apolello accepted. As I departed, Ana softly whispered to me, "may my Zapotec gods forever watch over you."

My adventure with the braceros—living, working, helping and sharing with them—added another dimension to my understanding of life in two cultures.

The Streets of East L.A.

As East Los Angeles became my stomping grounds, I passed from the tranquillity of a country village, Moorpark, to the hectic life of an urban barrio. From the moment I had stepped across the Los Angeles River into East L.A. in the 40s, it became my world, and except for a few brief absences, I have walked its streets for five decades.

Those first memorable days were spent under the ancient shade trees by lakes where families gathered, enjoyed picnics and children played under watchful, parental eyes. By the 60s, fantastic works of art–inspiring and colorful mosaics depicting the history of Mexican culture from the days of the Aztecs to the Revolution and beyond–would look down upon sidewalk crowds from business facades in the barrio. Everywhere, there were signs revealing the richness of our culture created by talented Chicano muralists, such as Carlos Almaraz, Gilbert Luján, Beto de la Rocha and Frank Romero.

This new world claimed my heart. On so many occasions, I would bring my mother from Moorpark, drive her over the Santa Suzana Pass and take her to the movie houses that played major Mexican films not available anywhere else. How happy it made her to see those films featuring performances by great Mexican stars, such as Pedro Armendariz, Carlos López Montezuma (El Chaflán), Mario Moreno (Cantinflas), Dolores del Río and Emilio Tuero.

My mother and I felt at home walking the streets of East Los Angeles in those early days. She loved the excitement of being with me. In Moorpark, she was subjected to her daily responsibilities, but here she was at liberty. And the people made her feel as if she were back in León.

Everywhere we went, there were Mexican clubs, restaurants and stores with signs proclaiming "*Se Habla Español*," that made it easy for my mother to understand. Later in the 50s, a huge market was built on First Street near Evergreen; called El Mercado, it colorfully replicated Jalisco's fabled atmosphere.

Lincoln Park would eventually become the home of Plaza de la Raza, a nationally recognized cultural center for the arts and education. Formerly known as Eastlake Park, the area was a favorite stop for travelers making the journey between the San Gabriel Valley and downtown Los Angeles. Its lakes covered eight acres. The park had been home to a zoo, an ostrich farm, a reptile farm and a motion picture studio. There was also a large horticultural conservatory filled with rare tropical plants. Visitors to Lincoln Park could find enjoyment on the miniature railway, the skating rink and the famous Lincoln Park Carousel.

As the centers of affluence moved to other parts of the city, a cloud of despair settled over what had by the 1940s become one of the most popular parks in the city. The carousel was destroyed by arson and the miniature zoo relocated to Griffith Park. Rowboats no longer plied the lake, and the boathouse, a community landmark for generations, was beginning to show signs of neglect. By the 1960s, the classic old red brick boathouse had been closed by the city and boarded up to crumble away. Fortunately for our community, Margo Albert, an actress, and others did much to make Plaza de la Raza a cultural highlight. In 1989, I paid Margo a much deserved tribute at the Century Plaza Hotel for her interest in giving her spare moments toward the creation of a landmark that is still such a source of pride for all of us.

Often, people ask me how it was that I came to be in East Los Angeles. I had, after all, been educated in Santa

Barbara and had grown up in a calmer community where my father had prospered as a business owner and in whose footsteps I could have followed. Just as the tumultuous aftermath of revolution in Mexico brought my parents to Moorpark, an outrageous miscarriage of justice that was being perpetrated against twenty-three Mexican Americans in the notorious Sleepy Lagoon case first attracted me to East Los Angeles.

The young defendants were charged with murdering a teenage boy at a ranch swimming hole where many youths of Mexican origin swam because city and county pools were closed to them. They were penniless and defenseless in a system that denied them even the most basic of human rights and dignity.

Their plight ignited such a tremendous spark in my soul that it opened my eyes to a new reality that would lead me down a different path than I had ever envisioned for myself. The injustices surrounding the Sleepy Lagoon incident were a shocking revelation to me about the depth and ferocity of racist feelings against the Mexican and Mexican American peoples. But another person I really wanted to meet was the heroic Alice Greenfield McGrath, a Jewish activist who almost single-handedly organized the defense of the Sleepy Lagoon victims.

A very young actor, Anthony Quinn, had also taken an interest in the case, along with Rita Hayworth and Orson Welles. I wanted badly to meet Mr. Quinn then, but it wasn't until 1975 that I finally sat down and talked with him. I told him, "Hey, Mr. Quinn, it took me thirty-five years to meet you."

After Sleepy Lagoon, I could not resist the temptation to be involved in East Los Angeles, and I found myself at the crossroads where, at last, the direction of my entire career became clear to me.

Although I would be proud to have had a personal involvement in the Sleepy Lagoon case, I did not. Nevertheless, it opened my eyes and showed me how, up to that time, my view of the world had been from the limited vantage point of an agricultural person from a small community. What concerned me was that there were many other cases like this that were covered up, never given the publicity this case had evoked. Now, I saw a bigger Mexican American world with serious problems which I felt an obligation to address and help resolve.

So it was that in the 40s, I adopted a cause that would occupy a lifetime. The challenge was clear and it involved the values that meant the most to me. I became determined to help my community make substantial changes. Here again, I was faced with uncertainty and it was apparent to me that the road ahead would be long and difficult.

In the beginning, under the imposing dome of a former Greek Orthodox Church, I became the first architect of the cultural and human services center on Euclid Square, known then as *La Casa del Mexicano*. Though *"la casa"* had no Mexican architectural motif, it served us well. La Beneficencia Mexicana, the mutual aid society which governed *la casa's* corporate policies, also called on me to be a member of its governing board. As it turned out, the elders of that organization thought of *beneficencia* as having to do more with furnishing sites for dances, social functions, baptisms and spending endless hours on mundane chores, such as fixing the plumbing. They were totally oblivious to the larger issues of community development. We ultimately parted ways when I kept bringing up the issues of immigration, health, welfare, housing, jobs and police brutality. Having voiced my opinion, I became a terribly controversial member. The group held a kangaroo court and ousted me for creating a disturbance by making what they considered to be radical public statements. I was quick to direct my volunteer services elsewhere.

As I got into the depth of activity in East Los Angeles in 1951 and 1952, I again ran into a hypocritical side of California's pretense of tolerance. The matter of anti-minority bigotry and anti-Mexican sentiment raised its ugly head against a backdrop of concern about a wave of police discrimination and brutality. Under the leadership of then State Senator Jack B. Tenney, an "American Plus" movement broke out. It was racist and xenophobic in spirit. The basic premise of the "American Plus" movement was similar to that of California's "Save Our State" hysteria of the mid '90s that threatened to deprive children of undocumented immigrants of health and education services through the passage of the infamous Proposition 187. The legislation urged by the "American Plus Movement" said it was intended to outlaw "un-American activities and all foreign influences with communistic inclinations." Members of the Sleepy Lagoon Defense Committee itself were grilled and then smeared in the press by Senator Tenney's inquisitors. Yet, it was nothing more than a legislative act supporting immigrant-bashing and, more specifically, Mexican-bashing.

Then California Attorney General Edmund G. (Pat) Brown (who would later become governor), said in his Lincoln Day address, "...you'd think Hitler or Stalin proposed it... this (proposal) moves this country back hundreds of years to bigotry, discrimination and persecution."

In 1955, I attempted to reason with the editorial staff of the *Los Angeles Times* to persuade them to change the course of negative media coverage of our community, which has been a major cause of our poor public image for more than a century.

I arranged a meeting with the then young Editor-Publisher, Otis Chandler. Reporters Rubén Salazar and

Eduardo Quevedo, accompanied me to that interview. We failed. Change for the better in coverage by the media would have to wait for decades.

Many Mexican American educators were furious that the schools in East Los Angeles showed little evidence of educational adaptation to the needs and potentials of our children. We felt alienated by the apparent insensitivity and the low expectations projected by instructors, counselors and administrators at the schools. On Lincoln's birthday in the auditorium of Lincoln High School in Lincoln Heights, the newly created Mexican American Opportunity Foundation sponsored a Mexican American parents' conference. Things broke loose after that.

The conference had called mass attention to the problem. In partial reaction to the conference, students organized the walkouts of the 60s, which were led by the heroic high school teacher, Sal Castro. In the beginning hours and days of the walkouts, the students had asked Castro to direct them to community activists who might provide leadership. He risked his professional life for our children. May his name be revered among America's twentieth century heroes.

During the height of this protest, a student committee came to me to see if I could arouse a response from President Johnson regarding their predicament, since they were aware that I had an appointment to the President's Committee on Community Relations. I had sat down with the students to explain to them how my organization, the Mexican American Opportunity Foundation (MAOF) might collaborate with them.

I immediately thought of contacting Attorney General Robert Kennedy, since I knew he was supporting the United Farm Workers Union in Delano. We finally located the Attorney General's party in the air en route to California.

Kennedy's pilot informed us that the plane would make a momentary stopover at a private airport near Los Angeles International, but warned that we would need special permission to meet with Kennedy. We contacted one of Kennedy's key aides, who listened to us and set up the meeting. He cautioned that the L. A. stopover would not exceed thirty minutes. "Don't be late," he said, "the plane cannot wait." He reserved only ten minutes for the Attorney General's dialogue with the boycotting students.

To their relief, the students and MAOF staff arrived before the plane landed. Robert Kennedy disembarked to meet with them, and the students explained the issues and their needs. Then Kennedy left, telling them not to worry. "We will do it together!" (My staff often repeats those words, "We will do it *togethah!*") To say that these young people were exhilarated is an understatement. Sadly, soon after, the day's promise was destroyed by an assassin's bullet.

The demand for change took root, however, and eventually the Mexican American students in the Los Angeles Unified School District felt they had an advocate on the school board in Dr. Julian Nava and in the later addition of two remarkable women pioneers of the cause, Leticia Quezada and Victoria Castro.

The educational issues finally hit a sensitive nerve and awakened our community. Other protests were to follow. The National Chicano Moratorium of August 29, 1970, expressed the massive opposition of youthful Mexican Americans to the further prosecution of the deadly and fruitless war in Vietnam. The war had already disproportionately claimed the lives of so many sons of East Los Angeles. The August protest march, which had drawn about twenty to thirty thousand participants from all around the country, had seemingly ended peacefully with a procession culminating in Laguna Park, which was later renamed in honor of journalist Rubén Salazar. That day, Rubén died, his skull shattered by an explosive gas shell fired by a Los Angeles County Deputy. Rubén's loss is still ingrained in my mind.

Since the streets had been cordoned off for the demonstration, I had made my way on foot along Whittier Boulevard from my office to where the crowd was thickest, unaware of the violence that was erupting in the park. While I was making my way through the crowded streets, I got as far as Indiana Street, when I got word of Rubén's death. I thought about how I used to get him to pick the avocados I couldn't reach in my own back yard. I'd say, "Since I don't have a tall *bracero* around to help me, I'll make you a deal: If you pick us some avocados, we'll split 50-50." I recalled the arguments about the term "Chicano," which he glibly defined as "Mexican Americans with Anglo images of themselves." But we agreed, more so than on any other topic, that the Chicano Movement found expression not only in a nationwide political awakening, but also in reinforcing the cultural roots of people of Mexican origin. At times, we would seem to be at each other's throats, but we never failed to calm down when the rhetorical storm had passed. Then, he would slowly walk off. With a bag of avocados in one hand, he would wave good-bye with the other.

Another of our constant discussions was about food. I have always cherished my favorite Mexican restaurants on César Chávez Boulevard, Whittier Boulevard and First Street. Each has its own delectable specialty, from menudo to *chiles rellenos* and *enchiladas.* I always search for places that offer the same tastes as my mother's cooking, a passion once shared by Rubén.

Once in a while, I would come across my pet peeve in a restaurant and often joke about it. That's when I would see on the menu "Spanish Omelette," "Spanish Rice" or "Spanish Tamale." I would tell the manager, "I'm not really in the mood for Spanish food. Do you have a Mexican tamale?" Rubén would tease the waitresses and ask them, "When a nice Gringo asks you what you are, how do you respond?" We were always disheartened when the answer was "I guess, I'm sort of a Spanish-speaking Latin, or whatever you want to call me." This ill-defined "twilight zone" of lost identity always seemed to us both to be a lame excuse for lack of clarity and pride in self-identity. I miss Rubén to this day.

The tragic rioting of that black day, following a peaceful march and the subsequent controversial inquest into Rubén's death, marked a turning point in the history of the Mexican American. The streets of East Los Angeles would never be the same. But I am still here.

The Birth of a Plan

The seeds for what would become my life's work were planted in Walnut Canyon. I had been looked upon, by our neighbors as a free-lance barrio counselor, an amateur advocate, a paralegal, an interpreter, and even a reviewer of important legal papers, such as the ever-complicated deeds to real estate and titles to cars. In short, I did not always have the solution, but I always earnestly looked for one. Sometimes, I would be on call for volunteer duty around the clock. Such crises, as a death in the family, a serious accident or illness, even an elopement, that could come at any time of day or in the dead of night often resulted in a knock on our door. My father would get me up and with great pride command me, *"¡Ayúdale!"* "Help him." I have always believed that I inherited this neighborhood role. *Consejo*, or advice, had been regularly sought from my grandfather.

There can be little doubt that my price was right. I never charged. But every Christmas would bring forth a chicken, a rabbit or a jar of apricot jam. This was one more experience that helped lay the groundwork for the steps I would eventually take in creating what was to become my career. These experiences led to the formation of the Mexican American Opportunity Foundation (MAOF).

In the early forties, I had become the youngest Notary Public in the history of Moorpark. My people thought that to be a Notary Public even in a small, sleepy town was a great achievement and extremely prestigious. That's the way it was in the Mexican culture.

The day came, however, when being a notary and a voluntary advocate were not enough. I resolved to move beyond long-winded discussions and into the world of solving our problems. There were no guidebooks available on how to provide bilingual social services. Conferences were held on the causal factors of unemployment, but the question of how to acquire actual jobs for thousands stagnated in a pool of unanswered questions. That is what led me to establish the MAOF.

My plan was about to get off the ground. It was my first opportunity to be an architect of a missing social structure, a designer of effective social machinery dedicated to the service of our people. I was to become part of a team that would put together an institution with its primary focus on getting our people out of dead-end jobs in the low-wage hole. As things began to unfold, I noticed that there was less and less criticism about the colossal task we were to tackle.

Throughout my life, the long, desolate search for real remedies has seemed almost hopeless at times. It was a shock to research the unutilized qualifications of our graduates from Stanford, Yale, Columbia, U.S.C. and other prestigious institutions. Among our people, even those with master's degrees, continued to be underemployed. The "good old boys club" was still in the way; and it still is.

It was not until 1960 that things started to happen and I began to study concrete examples of how I might proceed to put my plan to work. It was my goal to directly deliver the services so needed by many millions of Mexican-origin people who had languished, neglected in a deep, seemingly eternal well of poverty.

I studied the Jewish Federation as a conglomerate of human service agencies. To me it was a prime, national example of economic stability in human service delivery. I also studied the work of the Urban League, moving, as it did, toward the establishment of outreach offices to serve African Americans all over the nation. I was also privileged to confer with the famous Preacher-Congressman, Adam Clayton

Powell of Harlem. This colorful folk hero astounded me with his immediate help when he heard my appeal. He directed me without hesitation to Whitney Young, the National President of the Urban League. Mr. Young recognized my search for a way to do for my people what he and his distinguished predecessors had done for African Americans as the Civil Rights Movement got under way. He said in his gentle voice, "I will fill a wheelbarrow with paperwork, plans and designs for your community-based organization, so you will not have to waste your life reinventing the wheel!" I already had a small board of directors in place and now I needed to learn how to run a foundation.

Young saw me as an enthusiastic idealist in a heated search for pragmatic solutions. He knew that I was aware of great needs to be met and was desperately searching for the right tools for the job. This soft-spoken humanitarian and ethnic philosopher, who had been all over the world as a statesman, was able to articulate to me what his Urban League had accomplished, primarily in job training, housing and economic development. His words were a revelation to me. I absorbed them eagerly and sighed with a new feeling of comfort. He gave me the intellectual ammunition to fight for what I believed in. The critical point of his advice rested on his affirmation that it took a combination of great forces to accomplish what the Urban League had done: the community's own leadership, organized labor, corporate America and the political system. All had to work together.

The initial supporters of our Mexican American Opportunity Foundation had a placid environment in which to study and discuss options. The scene was the shady yard of my family home in Pico Rivera, a restored ranch acre, developed in 1913 on Shade Lane. Our home had once been the main house of a twenty-acre avocado orchard. The old tank tower

still stands. Growing there are thirty very old and still fruit-
ful avocado trees, the remnants of the former groves.

A group of us—Councilmen of Pico Rivera, Frank
Terrazas, Frank Macías, Tony Gallegos, Henry Alonzo, Jose
Montenegro and Charlie Ericksen—were involved from the
beginning. I was convinced that, in former years, my community had been plagued with too many "ends" and not enough
"means." It was true all across the Southwest. Our bubbling
stream of ideas, however, sank into the sand of endless
rhetoric. I promised myself I would not engage in the futility
of creating yet another pie-in-the-sky project. To me, the concept of harnessing powerful elements in the society to pull
the load of a massive program of service to a needy community represented the difficult road ahead. The plan we
developed envisioned a staff of trained, dedicated, bicultural
and bilingual experts who would provide human services
from virtually 6 a.m. to 6 p.m. every working day of the year.

At last, we began to feel confident with the ideas shared
by Whitney Young and others. We were on our way. After
five decades of struggle and twenty years of dedication to
the idea of creating a non-profit, community-based organization, we were finally developing the Mexican American
Opportunity Foundation. We dedicated it to the creation and
operation of programs dealing with our people in a language
they understood, with respect and cultural relevance.

We started very small and humble. An old friend gave us
a picturesque California bungalow which had formerly
housed a real estate office. Its style was typical of the small-
dwelling "bungalow" architecture of that period. The
building was located on the corner of Rosemead and
Whittier Boulevards in Pico Rivera. A couple of old desks, a
file cabinet and an ancient typewriter comprised our total
furnishings. My invaluable part-time assistant, even at that
time, Kathy Tafoya, made the curtains herself. We moved in

immediately and celebrated a "grand opening," complete with *mariachi, taquitos* and margaritas.

Sadly, the joy and comfort of having this new office was to be short-lived. Just seven days after moving in, a short circuit in the old electrical wiring caused a fire, which gutted the building. We lost everything we had. To be knocked out in the first round gave rise to arguments among my comrades in the cause. There were even some who urged us to forget the whole "damned idea." Realizing that I was still an amateur at organizing a community, I was determined not to "go down for the full count." I realized that the faint of heart rarely build anything notable. So I quickly recovered from my bruises and bounced back. That's when my converted garage in Pico Rivera became my first real, lasting office. It is, even today, a major operating site for proposals, strategy sessions, research and writing.

I started to raise funds, and a new battle surfaced. I had to confront apathy, indifference and even skepticism from some of our own community leaders. Many simply could not understand that qualified, professional staff had to be recruited and paid. Some asserted that I was merely trying to create a soft job for myself. Many were offended by any discussion of Mexican American problems, considering it harmful to the very dignity of the whole barrio. Even when Rubén Salazar editorialized in the *Los Angeles Times* advocating improvement of conditions affecting Mexican Americans in East Los Angeles, the Mexican Chamber of Commerce blasted him. The chamber even sent a delegation to meet with the publisher and demanded that Rubén be fired from the staff. In this environment, I began the long battle for comprehension of our cause by the contemporary leaders of corporate America. It's been an endless struggle ever since.

In my effort to build, I surrounded myself with people who were sympathetic with my beliefs. Sadly, many of these were unable to help me raise the money to cover the cost of the rent and telephone, least of all the high cost of meeting the payroll of a full-time professional staff. The process involved tremendous personal sacrifice: long hours, time spent away from my family and expenditure of what little personal funds I had in order to keep MAOF alive.

Anyone who starts a business from scratch—a gas station, a restaurant or a grocery store, for instance does it at great personal sacrifice. But, in this case, we were talking about a "people" business, what is known today as a human service institution. And there were no profits in terms of money to be made, only in the development of human potential.

At least, at this time of my life I had an answer to the Anglo diehards who always used to put me on the spot—those who would say, "If you Mexican Americans have so many problems, why don't you get together and solve them? Why don't you organize? Why don't you do something for yourselves? Why don't you do what other minorities have done? Stop bickering among yourselves and get some action going to solve your problems and help your own people." So, we finally gave them their answer. On February 7, 1963, a non-profit, community-based organization was born: the Mexican American Opportunity Foundation.

How disheartening it was between 1963 and 1965, when contributions from corporate America were so small that I had to beg my friends and acquaintances for anything from one dollar on up. During that time, I was a full-time employee of the Amalgamated Clothing Workers of America, in the garment industry, as a labor organizer. I devoted all my extra time to the foundation. My low wages combined with the money needed to run the foundation left little for my family.

My wife, María, also worked outside the home to help us make ends meet. My life's project might not have survived but for her support. The issue of sacrifice must not be minimalized. It really bruised my soul, especially affecting my self-esteem, not to be able to come home with a good paycheck. I went through periods of depression when I could not even buy cheap toys for my own children at Christmas and did not have any money to spend for a real family get-together. María never knew that on one weekend the money for the food we served was earned in payment for blood that I sold at a bloodbank on Los Angeles Street.

The increasing pressures started to control me and impose a frenetic pace on my life. The consequences gradually caused a certain distance to arise in my relationships with my children and my wife. For a while, there grew over my marriage a dimming of the light, as the space widened. However, our strong belief in family ties saved me from the total destruction of my home. The question became, "Who was to be my first love?" Was it to be my family or the ever increasing demands of the cause I had espoused and the people who surrounded me?

It was my wife's undying force of character that held things together against odds that would have defeated a lesser woman. If there has ever been a long-suffering and understanding person in my life, it is my wife, María. She has had the supreme patience to tolerate my divided devotion between home and my life's work.

She has an irresistible dry humor, which smooths the path of life endearingly. I recall that I came into the house one day, fresh from an awe-inspiring visit to the White House. I recounted to her all the distinguished personages I had met. Her response was, "That is all very interesting, I am sure, but the bottom line is that tomorrow is still trash day around here."

One of my charges as a federal officer when I was working for the Department of Agriculture was the examination of payroll accounts. María wondered out loud in her inimitable way how I could spot errors in a grower's payroll, but could not balance my own checkbook. She often referred to me as "Mr. America" when I would leave the house, bound for the office or a conference, dressed in executive attire, which contrasted sharply with the *bracero* attire I wore at home.

María has become a leader of parents throughout Southern California, sharing her expertise with other parents facing the challenge of raising a Down syndrome child, like my son Dionicio, Jr. Discovering his condition shook us both to our spiritual core. We received notice that our twins, Magdalena and Dionicio, Jr. were never going to be the same. The doctor advised us with paralyzing suddenness that "Chiefy" (my nickname for Dionicio, Jr.) had been diagnosed with Down syndrome. Chiefy is strong in heart, and husky as an ox. His gentle spirit has drawn our family together. What, at first, seemed a blow from which we might never recover, has become one of the greatest joys of our lives. When I come home from work each day, his is the face that I need to see. He is, at this writing, twenty-seven years old, and I cannot imagine my life without him.

As I finished my first draft of the first proposal for the foundation, I discussed it with my long-time friend, Juan Acevedo. Some considered him eccentric, but to others he was a wise East Los Angeles counselor and grass-roots leader. When it came to community activism and discussion of community issues, he was generally considered the one to consult, especially in the 50s. He had graduated from UCLA and was long recognized as a prime Chicano sociologist. To many, his philosophical views seemed tremendously valuable. To me his advice fell short. For a man so sought after, I was appalled at how pessimistic he was. But, his mind-set was common for the time. Still, I was startled to hear him say, "You have too many strikes against you to succeed at such a formidable task. First," he exclaimed, "you are too dark a Mexican to create such an organization. You talk about going to the White House (they're just going to slam the door in your face.) Looks are very important in this business. Why, you don't even own a decent suit of clothes." Regrettably, he was right about the clothes.

In the loudest tones he could command, he bellowed, "We, Mexicans, are very disorganized!"

I could never accept that we were born to be disunited. Being poor contributes to our disunity. For a moment, my world stood still as I pondered the depths of his unvarnished judgement.

He ran on still further: "You're a damned Indio who insists on beating a silent drum." He was more than emphatic when he said, "Forget it, You'll never make it fly. Get these foolish delusions out of your system."

I had come to him full of hope, and all he could say in the spirit of brotherhood was, "You are an old fool, full of baloney."

Little did he realize that he placed a challenge before me that would inspire me even more. So, to Juan, my friend, in spite of it all, I will be forever indebted. His words of discouragement worked in the opposite way. In the long run, I feel I proved him wrong.

On reflection, I have often felt disgruntled and unfulfilled because of things that fell through the cracks, because of opportunities forever lost by apathy. Outwardly, I have covered these feelings with a reflexive smile. Often, those who work at my side interpret this facial expression as a sign of general contentment. But to say that I have been immune from depression in the major setbacks of my life would be a gross mis-statement. So, once in a while, when I drive down Third Street to Belvedere Park, and view Dionicio Morales Plaza with its colorful dedication sign, I stop for a while to sit by the lake and feed the ducks. It is a symbol of Los Angeles County's appreciation of the benefits our Foundation's programs have rendered to the people of East Los Angeles. The plaza was dedicated to me in 1990. It is good to be appreciated while one is still around to hear about it. In my acknowledgements at the dedication, I remarked that "parks are usually named for people who have died," I, just the same, am happy to be around to enjoy it.

L.B.J. to the Rescue

Two years of trying to raise money for the foundation proved fruitless. To complicate matters, the ten people who had been with me through this struggle decided to give it all up. It was the consensus that we had exhausted our resources.

I didn't think so. Like any good leader, I faced either retreat or advance. I pleaded for just one more chance.

Frank Terrazas gruffly asked, "What do you propose to do?"

"We haven't talked to the President of the United States yet," I answered.

We had not yet had the opportunity to present our case to John Fitzgerald Kennedy. They all burst out in laughter. My team wondered if I had lost my marbles. To them, it all seemed beyond our reach.

Someone asked, "How do you propose to get in touch with him?"

I could feel my blood pressure rising. I got lightheaded. My heart was pounding. It now, was do or die. My answer struck my associates like a bombshell. In a trembling voice, I said, "Why not call him on the phone?"

At that moment, it was noon in Pico Rivera and 3:00 p.m. in Washington, D.C. The idea of calling J.F.K. personally seemed like a mission impossible. Even that was some relief to the general malaise of the meeting, which some thought would result in dissolving our ineffective organization. All we had left to show for our struggle was $22 in the treasury and two copies of our constitution and bylaws. In a moment of desperation and in the presence of ten skeptical board members, I picked up the phone, dialed the White House and spoke to a woman on the switchboard. "To whom do you wish to speak?" she asked. When I said, "To the President, please," there was a pause. At this point, ten stunned board members were staring at me, blankly. She asked the nature of my call.

I said that I was from a Mexican American group in Pico Rivera, interested in talking about doing something about the employment problems of our people.

She referred me to the Mexican Embassy in Washington and gave me the number. She kindly advised me that the ambassador might resolve my problem.

At this point, it almost seemed like the end of the road. I dialed again and the ambassador's secretary heard my story and said, "I think that the ambassador is meeting with Vice-President Lyndon Johnson at this moment about the concerns you have expressed." She then advised me to call the Vice-President and gave me his number. I called once more and was referred to one of L.B.J.'s chief deputies. When I asked to speak with Mr. Johnson, he was pleased to hear from a person with my interests. He told me that there would be a Conference on Equal Employment Opportunity and that Mr. Johnson was the Chairman of the President's Committee on Equal Employment Opportunity. I was further informed that L.B.J. would be glad to talk to me personally before the conference to discuss Mexican American employment issues, as they were looking to someone from the west coast to participate in the conference.

As a result of the phone conversation, I received a formal telegram of invitation repeating the offer of a special audience with the Vice-President.

Of course, I had no money for the transcontinental trip. But our committee of ten, now with renewed hope, got together the price of the ticket. I was left to worry about the specifics of my out-of-pocket expenses along the way. With about $15 in my wallet, I arrived in Washington, D.C., the day before my appointment and spent the night in an all-night movie house, watching and rewatching *"Fort Apache,"* with John Wayne. The satchel-style briefcase I carried was borrowed for the occasion to carry my proposal. Inside the satchel, my wife had packed a toothbrush, a pair of shorts and some socks. I had added two bananas. When I went for my mother's blessing, she added to the briefcase three burritos wrapped in Weber's Bread wax paper. In the morning, after a shave in the Pickwick Bus Station, I announced my presence to the Vice-President from a phone booth. When asked where they should pick me up, I asked a man shining shoes what hotel was nearby. He said, "The Capital Hilton." That is where they picked me up.

Before the conference started, I had the opportunity to meet with L.B.J. I recall two memorable features of the man; the first was his firm, powerful handshake and the second his very marked Texas drawl. I asked him for just seven minutes of his time. He greeted me with that unforgettable Texas-style handshake and said, "You can have seventeen!"

L.B.J. opened the conversation with an expression of his concern that Mexican American people rarely sought him out, even though his position as Chairman of the President's Committee on Equal Employment Opportunity put him in a position to be of help.

I told him, "I have a proposal for the Department of Labor. I've been sent all over the place and nothing happens. They tell me in Los Angeles to go to the Urban League. Will you help me get it funded?"

L.B.J. asked, "May I see it?"

Of all the times to go through an embarrassing predicament, I couldn't open the briefcase. Mr. Johnson's secretary tried to rescue me with the aid of a letter opener. Meanwhile,

L.B.J. took it all in with patience and grace, smiling. Suddenly, the briefcase flew open. Out rolled my socks, the three burritos, the bananas and my underwear. The cascade of personal items rolled across the office floor and under the Vice President's desk. When I crawled under the desk to retrieve them, the secretary joined me and whispered in my ear, "Please don't be embarrassed. He's used to this sort of thing!" Despite my embarrassment, I was finally able to hand the Vice-President of the United States my proposal. It got to the Department of Labor and it got funded.

This was the beginning of my long friendship with L.B.J. On various occasions, L.B.J. called on me. When the time came for the U.S. to return the disputed El Chamisal to Mexican sovereignty, Mr. Johnson invited me to join the official delegation which restored the title of the land to Mexico. He was always gracious and attentive and seemed to intuitively appreciate the depths of frustration which lay behind my emotional appeal for help.

There was another immediate outcome of my first interview with L.B.J. It happened that during our interview, Mr. Johnson asked, "Dionicio, is there anything else I can do to help?"

I asked, "Is there a photographer around? Unless I take a photograph home with me, sir, none of my buddies will believe that I was here with you!"

After the photograph was taken and I was walking out the door, he once again said, "What else can I do for you?"

This was another opportunity that I just couldn't let pass up. My response to L.B.J.'s question was an invitation to the Vice-President to come to Los Angeles as my guest on an official visit to be honored by our Mexican American community. It would be an opportunity for him to get to know us, to assess our needs in person and to establish a permanent dialogue with our leadership with a view to improving conditions.

The news reached Los Angeles ahead of me. Literally hundreds of the most important leaders of the Mexican American community responded to my call for a precedent-setting meeting at the Los Angeles Hilton with the Great Texan. Ironically, in the community-wide whirlwind of preparatory activities and political squabbling, freelancing barrio politicians, frantic to get into the limelight, muscled in on the arrangements to such an extent that it was hard for me to keep control of the preparations. After all, in those days how many times did such a distinguished White House visitor accept an invitation to a local conference?

When the long-awaited day came at last, we watched unfold one of the most important events in the long history of Los Angeles and of the Mexican Americans in the Southwest. The setting was the Pacific Ballroom in the Los Angeles Hilton, filled to overflowing with 1,200 leaders of the Mexican American community of Los Angeles and California. At the podium was the massive, human diamond in the rough: Lyndon Baines Johnson.

When Johnson began to speak, the effect was electric. The conversation at the more than one hundred crowded banquet tables fell silent. The organ tones of that deep Texas drawl and that winning smile were hypnotic. No tinkle of silverware or glasses disturbed the reverence for the speaker. In a few hypnotic sentences, the man who had risen from the banks of the Pedernales to the banks of the Potomac won a profound rapport with his listeners.

At this spine-tingling moment of awe and expectation, Johnson dropped a bombshell. He asked, "My fellow Americans, can you guess how many communications I have received from the total Mexican American and Hispanic population of the United States during the several months I have been in office as Chairman of the Presidential Committee on Equal Employment Opportunity? How many do you think? 1,000? 10,000? 20,000?" There was a pause. Many thought that L.B.J.'s daily mail must be heavy with reports from the millions of Mexican Americans specifying conditions of discrimination and unfairness in employment. Then came the bombshell. Johnson answered his own question: "Sixty-five!" Many thought he must have meant 65,000. But no, sixty-five! Many shook their heads in disbelief.

Johnson gently chided his listeners on the almost total lack of communication on the part of Mexican Americans nationwide with functionaries of government who would be in a position to help in civil rights and equal opportunity in employment.

Johnson traced his deep interest in the improvement of conditions for Mexican Americans to his early years as a teacher in a one-room, "Mexican" school in the Rio Grande Valley. He told how he had taken out money from his meager salary of $40 per month to buy some simple playground equipment and repair the broken windows in that neglected schoolhouse. He also said, "I remember with great fondness how a Mexican family took me in to eat noon meals when I was broke."

As I sat beside him at the head table, I could literally feel the depth of his emotion and the utter sincerity of his desire to be of service in combating the discrimination that sat like a heavy burden on the shoulders of his Mexican American fellow citizens. When he concluded his remarks, there was hardly a person in the audience who doubted that Johnson would use the power of his position to help us.

Vice-President Johnson was as good as his word, and his close relationship with the Mexican American leadership in the Los Angeles area produced many positive results through the years. But the euphoria of that great meeting at the Hilton was soon dispelled for me, personally, by the sudden intrusion of the realities of life.

In the tragic aftermath of the assassination of President John F. Kennedy, L.B.J. became president. Soon, another wire came for me from the White House. It announced my appointment to the President's Committee on Community Relations and it concluded with an invitation for me to attend the White House Rose Garden ceremony of installation of the members of the commission.

I imagine that any person would be thrilled to receive an invitation to the White House. But it was special for me because, in the early 60s, I was one of the first Mexican Americans ever appointed to any type of national commission. How proud my people were that I was appointed! How symbolic my appearance there would be! I told all my relatives and friends the good news. But I hadn't reckoned with my boss. At that time, I was still working for the Amalgamated Clothing Workers Union.

I was not prepared for what happened when I asked my supervisor for permission to take two days off to go to the White House. I thought he might feel honored that one of his employees, a member of the staff of his union, had been so recognized. Instead, I received a bitter, devastating disappointment. My boss's answer was kindly delivered, but, nonetheless, it was a slap in the face: "Permission denied. We need you here on the job; we don't pay you to wander around all over the country."

The message was clear. My lips got dry. I felt an empty sensation in my heart. I thought how lucky I had felt when some community leaders made the necessary plans and provided hotel expense money for my trip. Now I wouldn't need it. It seemed clear to me that if I went to Washington in defiance of orders, I would lose my job. It crossed my mind that my boss actually wished that he had been the one selected for the honor of an invitation to the White House. I never got to the Rose Garden to be installed. The lost opportunity and the dividends of that trip in human dignity and pride for our people were lost.

Having experienced so many disappointments throughout my previous years, I just accepted it as one more blow, as I had so many others. Then, I recalled that so many other Mexican Americans had survived thousands of such galling experiences. The battle was just beginning.

A History of MAOF Programs

A red letter day came when one man, actor Steve Allan, changed the whole level of our financial support. He gave us our first sizable contribution—a check for $500. What an ecstatic moment that was! No one had ever given us $500. I then used Steve Allan's check in my corporate solution.

Among my first corporate visits, I singled out a major Los Angeles aerospace firm which boasted of its equal opportunity policies. Here we were in the first years of the national excitement over equality—which had been Lyndon Johnson's brainchild—and I was jolted to find that Presidents and C.E.O.s knew little and cared very little about the work-force potential of Mexican Americans, least of all in administrative positions.

When I visited the aerospace company, I was given a guided tour of the plant. I remember telling the president that I had encountered no brown faces among the hundreds of employees I had seen during the tour, not even janitors.

He replied, "The janitors come in at night."

When I asked to meet a Vice-President or any other high-ranking official of Mexican descent, he averted his eyes and said, "I guess we don't have any. But we're training them."

That was 1965. I asked, "Aren't you an equal opportunity employer?"

With no hesitation and without giving any sign of discomfort at my challenge to his employment policies, he avoided my question and told me that he had become a great admirer of the comparatively few Mexicans he had chanced to observe. He said that at the exclusive Jonathan Club, where he occasionally lunched with other executives, the waiters were all handsome and extremely courteous Mexicans. As a matter of fact, he was learning Spanish from the waiters. Then, in all seriousness, he explained that since his corporation was not in the food service business, he could not hire waiters. As he traveled to the races at Del Mar by train, he said that he had seen many Mexican track workers. They seemed like very hardworking people. To emphasize his goodwill, he boasted about his frequent fishing weekends in Ensenada and the good *enchiladas* he had there.

He had never heard that there were many lawyers, judges and engineers among us.

Ironically, when I returned to that corporation twenty years later, the C.E.O. informed me they were still in the process of training Mexican Americans for supervisory positions. The same old story. But this time, they did introduce me to a Latin technician from Argentina who looked like Bob Hope.

Almost every executive I met in that period seemed to be blind to our needs and rights. Often, I would be invited to the fifty-first floor and receive promises of commitments to hire our people. Like many before me, I would be disappointed, because when it came to communicating the promises made on the 51st floor to the first floor—where the personnel office was located—the message had already been lost. In the 60s, I found only scattered willingness on the part of industry or government to give the employment needs of the Mexican American any priority whatsoever. In that day as now, "minority" meant "African-American."

The economic problems of the barrios were increasing in both magnitude and complexity. It was evident in those days that we would have to literally thrust aside the obstacles between us and equal employment opportunity. We still had to show corporate employers that they had been remiss in waiting so long to tap the vast reservoir of skill and talent that was ours. In my many years of job hunting for my people, I never really felt that Affirmative Action worked for us at all.

Since our forefathers had possessed the talent and even the genius to conceive and build the pyramids of Teotihuacán, the cathedrals of colonial times and the Aztec engineering marvels of great dams and aqueducts and even to search the heavens to make the greatest calendar ever invented in the Western Hemisphere, then certainly we were justified in striving for a place in the modern world of technology and creativity in the twentieth century!

I submitted an endless series of job proposals, some through the support of Lyndon Johnson. Finally, the historic day came when the United States Department of Labor awarded us funds for on-the-job training of 400 worker aspirants. At this point, the stars began to shine brightly in our direction. because of that program, we successfully placed hundreds of trainees in entry-level jobs. They came from the barrios of East Los Angeles, the vineyards of the San Joaquin Valley and the lettuce fields of Salinas. Washington was stunned by our success. Within a year, we were rewarded with funding for 1375 trainees and later for 1700! We covered the entire Los Angeles metropolitan area with our recruitment of trainees. They needed relevant instruction in a language they understood. And the results pleased employers! As a result, I became the first Mexican American with a million-dollar contract. Many skeptics became believers. It was 1968.

The pace of our activities began to gather momentum. Hundreds of the people in our job training programs were quickly absorbed into the workforce. This was happening in a community that had been suspicious about the far-reaching goals that I had preached for years to the East Los Angeles barrios. Every time we placed another skilled work-

er, word got around, because they were being hired by corporations that had never before hired a Mexican American!
We had passed a major milestone in the nation's history
of equal job opportunity. I recall that our first experiment in
job training went so well that people began to look at the
foundation as a catalyst for getting a job or finding a better
one. MAOF simply meant jobs to them. People even began
to dream of getting promoted to supervisory levels of
responsibility through MAOF training. Many of our successful trainees returned to us requesting guidance for
acquiring supervisory rank. They were being passed over by
others who they felt had less preparation. Some even
aspired to policy-making positions, which at that time was
inconceivable to the majority. I felt proud as a peacock on
the rare occasions when I was able to place a trainee in a
high-tech job.

Our little two-room headquarters on Brooklyn Avenue,
now César Chávez Boulevard, could hardly contain our
exciting growth. We found a larger locale in the El Hoyo
section of East Los Angeles. Then, in the '90s, we were able
to purchase a spacious site in Montebello, a suburb of Los
Angeles. A three-acre site of a famous girls' high school.

In our early days, we were a welcome alternative to
those who dreaded the frustration of visiting the California
Department of Employment office. We began to make history by placing our people with such large corporations as
Rockwell, Northrop, Kraft, Hughes, McDonnell Douglas, the
Gas Company and Southern California Edison. We set up a
bridge to this new world of opportunity, where our people
could cross over without fear of being turned down.

Two problem areas affected what, for us, was the virgin
territory of Mexican American placement in large corporate
environments. One was that many of our people still felt
that a job in these great companies was "not for them." The

second hurdle was tests. I was troubled by the probability that the tests served to keep us out of the better jobs. What drove me up the wall was to encounter so many promising applicants, fully qualified, except in the matter of test-passing for eligibility. Since then, we have made instruction in test-taking an integral part of our program.

A question was once asked of me regarding what the MAOF had been doing for the elderly. I discovered that the old people of Mexican descent in California were being neglected. I found out that the Department of Labor had funds for part-time work for elders, and immediately negotiated funds to serve our "over 55" population in Oxnard, Bakersfield and East Los Angeles. We actually provided elders with four hours per day of work. I preferred to offer job rehabilitation rather than part-time recreation.

I still feel good when I get to talk at the elders' monthly luncheons. I am impressed with the transformation of many who had wiled away many of their years in tattered clothes and loneliness; now they are dressed in suits and find life after 55 to be great.

Despite these early successes, everything seemed hard in those start-up days. As I moved toward revising the MAOF board to bring in more representation from corporate America, there was suddenly a heartbreaking backlash from my people. I had started to honor corporate personalities for their contributions and, subsequently, appointed some of them to the Board of Directors of the MAOF. At our first Aztec Awards at the Los Angeles Hilton in 1969, young Mexican American picketers held signs that read, "Morales *es un vendido*" (Morales is a sellout). Many of those who protested were activists from the Chicano Movement. They found a way to attack the insensitivities of corporate America—I could hardly disagree. But I had already succeeded in getting jobs for our people. It was very difficult for me to accept such an attack directed at me. How ironic that the one key that would give strength to the fiscal base of a foundation that I had just barely put together would be harshly criticized by the very people it was founded to help. It was hard to realize that after I had spent years educating corporate employers to our needs and pleading with them to give, I was to be chastised by those I was committed to help.

Without knowing whether to react with anger or disdain, for months I bled inside.

My Grandfather's Insights Reborn

When our Mexican American Opportunity Foundation started its successful drive to make job placements of women, especially women who were single parents, the problem of what to do with their children became a concern. Subsidized childcare was the answer. We were convinced that once we started the program, cultural education would be an important educational goal, since we had decided we would serve only barrio children. Through the multi-purpose child-care program, we hoped, we would have a method of breaking the endless cycle of welfare dependency. An astonishing revelation was that we could find no professional experts on culturally relevant early childhood education. There was scarcely any literature to consult and almost no teacher training institution to show us how to develop such an idea.

I had often been drawn back to the memory of my first days of school. They were unforgettable days of real fear. Later, when I had learned to call it trauma, I could not let go of the idea that someday I would be able to prevent other children from continuing to experience the horrors of my own first years of schooling.

I wondered what had been different about my life that, of all my classmates of Mexican heritage, I alone had graduated from high school in 1937. My answer was that pride in my identity was constantly reinforced. The fascinating stories my grandfather told me as a child made all the difference for me. I had survived with minimal frustration, and I had begun to become more conscious of who I was, even if my Anglo teachers and schoolmates had no idea what my life was all about.

In the early 1970s, we were funded to develop child care centers. Then we were confronted with a question: "How could we design a program that would be geared to children with language limitations?" Some spoke only English, others only Spanish and a few were, to different degrees, bilingual. The answer was a bilingual/bicultural program. We created our own bilingual program. Communication was established in the child's first language and progressed to fluency in English and Spanish. The children would hear stories about the splendors of Mexican culture, how rubber and chocolate were discovered, for instance. Children would dance and sing the regional songs of their forefathers. But we were true pioneers in establishing an inter-generational program. The children would learn arts and crafts as taught by grandparent volunteers. We would supplant the inflexibility and insensitivity of pre-school education with sensitivity and flexibility. We would give the children the gift of self-esteem that my grandfather had given me. And that is how it has been since then.

In those early days, I found myself continually defending that part of our pre-school education that would be centered around a culturally-oriented program. It was misperceived by some as Mexicanizing the children rather than telling them the vital truth about who they were: Americans.

How can the study and experience of other cultures make one a better rounded, happier and more useful American? It was no mystery to me. How could forgetting one's first culture and language damage the children and the adults they would become? That was the question. Slowly, a few began to understand.

In the early 1970s, I was invited to speak at a conference of early childhood educators. I spoke from my heart and experience. I told them how our innovative methods were working, how we were instilling pride and self-esteem.

In that speech, I declared that, "Anyone presuming to teach Mexican American pre-school children and to receive state and federal money for it, with no special preparation or cultural sensitivity, is cheating our children." I lost standing with many in my audience. The response to that speech was... nothing. It was as if, during my talk, the volume had been turned down and no one had heard me.

I had naively expected someone to say, "Mr. Morales, those are challenging thoughts, worth thinking about." That did not happen. There was only silence as I spoke about the burgeoning Mexican American child population.

Kay Witcher, my dear friend in the Child Development Division of the Department of Education, who in that early period had understood the importance, the goals and the rightness of what we were doing, encouraged me to persist. She urged me to continue to say what I had to because one day people would begin to listen. Fear of change would dissipate, and they would at last be able to hear.

To offset the image of inferiority projected upon us by those who blindly followed the old patterns of racism or who were simply unaware of our plight, we were convinced we had to develop a battery of innovative techniques. The matter of cultural reinforcement would become a powerful tool in the hands of the teachers of our children in their most formative years.

We had come full circle. In seeking to widen the horizons of Mexican American women, to give them a broader spectrum of occupational choice and a chance to earn more money, we had come across a totally unploughed field of need: the field of systematic, culturally sensitive early childhood preparation. Our children would enter elementary school with unfettered expectations for success in school and in life.

No matter where I go, this question inevitably pops up: "Aren't there more than a hundred ethnic groups in the L. A. area with unmet needs? Why not take the multicultural approach?" Apart from the fact that I am always pointing out that my own experience in life has been Mexican American and that I know and feel our needs first-hand, I must say that the demographic facts of the Los Angeles County's Supervisory District One confirmed to me that we are meeting a pressing need. District One is among the areas that exemplify the greatest need for these services in the nation. Simply put, we have more children here than in any other district in the Los Angeles County. There are more than 170,000 Latino children in District One, of whom 90% are Mexican American! For every Anglo child there are more than eight Latino children. For every Black child, there are thirty-one Latino children. For every Korean child, there are 154 Latino children, and for every Laotian child there are 1900 Latino children.

Although we recognize and value this diversity, many of us feel that our primary obligation is determined by the needs of the clear majority, who are of Mexican descent. Mexican American and other Latino children suffer the greatest educational deprivations, and they are the poorest.

⤜

Thank you, my grandfather, Don Lorenzo, for being my best professor. Your legacy can be seen in all of our child-care centers.

Job Training Behind Bars

Late one evening, I found myself sleepily watching an old black and white Cagney movie about the sterility of human life in prison. It was then that I began to envision thoughts of how I might bring some light into the forsaken world behind bars. Sadly, that was one scenario in which our people were well represented. But the overall concern I had was not so much their serving time, but how they could survive on the outside upon release. It was all about jobs. Every inmate I talked to yearned for one supreme break: a good job waiting on the outside.

I continually received countless letters from inmates requesting my assistance in seeking job opportunities that could shorten their time in prison. But the commitment I would have to make called for an actual job, ready and waiting for the applying ex-offender. It was this realization that brought me to design a program that could help them to never return to their cells.

I got a chance to air my ideas to a bright assemblyman, at this writing, a Los Angeles city councilman, Richard Alatorre. With his enthusiastic support, we were able to persuade the State of California to make available one million dollars for a three-year period. Our training program would operate in the correctional facility at Susanville, in northern California.

Thus, began the partnership between the Mexican American Opportunity Foundation and California's Department of Corrections. Richard Alatorre, by standing with us and using his political leverage, won the gratitude of all the inmates.

In the ensuing weeks, we put together a lesson plan that would excite and stimulate the trainees. I enjoyed the brainstorming it entailed. It became evident that three basic educational objectives were appropriate for the Mexican American ex-offenders to succeed upon release. This was the rationale of the state's decision to fund us. We would train for real jobs; we would identify and develop employers who would give them a chance and hire them; and we would give them money to live on while they waited for their first paycheck. We also kept an eye on them and were ready to respond to any problems they might have, especially when they went to their first interviews.

That first visit to Susanville seemed like a movie version of life-behind-bars come true. There were the metal detectors with women visitors removing all the pins from their hair. There was a menacing tower in a narrow area between two tall fences. It was chilling to see the guards looking down with rifles at the ready. Like a robot, I walked through the clattering iron doorways.

That first day "behind the walls," I met with inmate leaders and the administration. Every discussion, repeated over and over, revolved around the absence of training for real jobs on the outside and the need for someone to develop those skills in time for their release. My response was always that we were prepared and equipped to do something about this. But the prospective trainees were still skeptical. They didn't trust me. One said, "Don't give us this bullshit." The contract provided that our program focus was to be on Mexican American inmates, whose goal became rehabilitation during their incarceration.

Our program was new, but it ran so well that what was planned as a three-year program was extended to a full four years. The classrooms were located within the walls.

Instruction was directed by a daring young educator, Tino Martínez.

Our subsequent success showed up spectacularly. There had been a 94% job placement and only 9% recidivism during the four-year period of operation of the program. This compared to 30 to 50% job placement and 60 to 70% recidivism experienced nationwide. In every speech I gave, talking about the results we had achieved, I said, "I never imagined this would exceed my greatest expectations." Such a record had been previously unheard of. We had made history in the eyes of the public and in the annals of correctional science in the State of California. However, I had to fight a couple of board members who vehemently opposed MAOF's involvement with this program. They said it gave MAOF "a bad reputation."

That many corporations sent their representatives to participate in the training program proved to be a powerful incentive and began to change the attitudes of non-believers. It began to dawn on the inmates that the world beyond the walls had moved on technologically. So our pilot program got off the ground with computer training, innovative multimedia classroom presentations and carefully selected job-related curriculum. All of this was not new to us, because we had already invested years of experience in East Los Angeles. We had learned to train in terms of workplace actualities and to circumvent dead-end jobs. Our trainees had no time to waste.

What appeared to be an impossible task began to excite the desolate inmates. Although some of our trainees had awesome rap sheets, they became very motivated by our program. They did their homework. They were so impressed with what we were doing for them that every time I dropped in on my monthly visit, I noticed an unforeseen level of courtesy and respect for me.

On one occasion, I asked a very handsome young inmate, who might well have qualified by his looks for a screen part, why he was serving time. He responded in a low monotone that he was serving seven years for killing his "old lady." He had found her in bed with another. This was the quiet, communicative and accepting way with which I was treated. I had won them over.

However, the horror stories of how they interacted among themselves were difficult to forget. Many of them made no bones about hating the black inmates and about how they would win the next battle inside the cold prison walls. They talked to me freely about prostitution among themselves and how they would guard their lovers.

One of the most exciting courses we offered, it seemed to me, was the training for Xerox Office Machine Repair. Dozens of ex-offenders are still happily employed today in this lucrative occupation. Many of them learned their survival skills, "how to live when you get out" and how to perform on the job from our program.

As the inmates were released, a fine-tuned network of "inside" and "outside" staff came into play. We picked up the newly released at the bus station, took them to our office and found housing for many of them. C and R Clothiers provided us with hundreds of suits of clothes. Sears came up with massive donations of shirts, ties and underwear. Our job developers in East Los Angeles accompanied them to their first day of work, introducing them to their employers. In that way, we softened the psychological trauma of the first interview.

These same job developers were alert to condition employers beforehand to set aside their attitudes about ex-offenders as future employees. That was not an easy task! This was the most exciting challenge of the program. But we would tell the employers of the ex-offenders' efforts to be worthy of a second chance, and we even offered ourselves as guarantors of the full rehabilitation of these trainees. The art of sensitizing employers in corporate America was the crux of all our workshops for program improvement. Our job developers were not only friends, but effective advocates during these critical days.

Unfortunately, with all its promise, the program survived only four years and then was allowed to die a painful death as a result of the passage of Proposition 13, a state referendum which halted all increases in property taxes. In the face of what we had learned and proven, the nation's policies on "correction" continued to favor the multiplication of prison facilities rather than the development of relevant rehabilitation.

Right before the program died, after all the laborious and labyrinthine bureaucratic preparations we had endured to establish our daring and innovative program at Susanville, and after all the success stories testifying to the lives we had restored, an unforeseen glitch surfaced. The district attorney at Susanville charged me with being too soft in dealing with the incarcerated trainees. He thought I was involved in something shady. He called for an investigation. He was running for re-election at the time and tried desperately to make political hay out of our job-readiness program. I spent many a sleepless night trying to figure out how to deal with this attack.

Luckily for me, I had on our board of directors at MAOF a deputy district attorney of Los Angeles County, Carlos Borja, who traveled to Susanville with me and quickly resolved the wild obstructionist allegations that were being made against our program.

Without the security that only a job can give our people, the nation will continue to face the frustration of costly mass incarceration. Crime, after all, is largely a response to the nation's failure to invest in job training rather than prison construction. I wish that I could say that we still operate this program. I still receive letters from some trainees who are no longer behind bars. I believe that we gave them hope where only despair had reigned. But the lack of funding has eliminated the same hope for others.

As I reflect on the many programs that I have been privileged to develop, I find this one to be one of the most rewarding. The letters, phone calls and personal visits all reinforce the sentiment–profound gratitude for my role in helping re-direct their lives. The feeling I get from hearing those two words, *Muchas gracias*, is hard to beat.

Sí, Se Puede

My pilgrimage of the heart has taken me from the fabulously rich Valley of the San Joaquin to the world famous lettuce fields of Salinas and the southern gateway of California at San Ysidro.

Our cause has led me from the sidewalks of East Los Angeles to the lofty citadels of corporate power and from the precincts of the Rio de Los Angeles to the White House on the far off banks of the Potomac.

We have built a state-wide chain of bi-cultural child care centers for the youngest of us, promoted corporate employment for Mexican American applicants at every level of technology, set up training programs for the unskilled and invaded penitentiary walls to bring hope and saleable skills to reformed offenders.

I have defended the rights of women. I have joined with others to fight an unprecedented wave of Mexico-bashing with every resource at my command. I have particularly enjoyed finding jobs for our elderly and joining them in the fun things they so like to do. All of this, daily emanating from our MAOF corporate headquarters in a beautiful suburb of East Los Angeles, with an annual budget of $20 million, 322 full-time employees, 25 programs and 23 outreach offices.

My son, Tim, who runs our Family Resource Center in Orange County, is sometimes discouraged by the lack of enthusiasm and motivation among many of the people in our own community and among those with influence and power, and by the lack of sufficient funding to pursue the mission of the foundation.

"But Tim," I say, "this has been our story from day one!"

We often debate the difference between oratory and the actual delivery of services. And, our discussions all wind up with the immortal Cesar Chavez's optimistic affirmation:

"Sí, se puede!"

The Glorious Day

Here I am again, relaxing to the rhythms of my favorite *mariachi* CD under my old avocado tree, working on some notes for a speech. Here, in this tranquil little corner of my world, I have passed so many pleasant hours over the last forty years.

The MAOF was born in the relaxing atmosphere of this open-air think tank, where our first rough blueprints of the future were put together. Oh, how we did argue—for hours! I can still hear the echoes of those heated debates among MAOF's pioneers. They were about how to get our project off the ground.

It is Saturday afternoon and three of my great-grandchildren are playing around me. They all bear proud Aztec names: Cuauhtemoc, who is five years old, Ehecatl, age eight and Altair, age nine. It is late autumn and the branches overhead are heavy with bright green avocados. As Cuauhtemoc climbs and reaches for an unripe avocado, I teasingly warn him, "They're not ready to pick yet." I know it doesn't really matter, after all; the picking is not to eat, but for something to throw at each other. Instead, I toss the children my son's old soccer ball. They easily switch their game. The game would have been marbles when I was their age. As they play, I envision the roles they are destined to fill in the first century of a new millennium. In that flash of introspection, I begin to worry.

I ask myself: By 2020, will they still feel the need to hide a proud heritage with a name change? Will they still prefer Latino, Hispanic, Spanish American, or evade the proud terms Mexican and Mexican American? I hope not!

My optimism cannot but envision that early in the twenty-first century, the scapegoating of us will have ceased. My whole spirit rejects the idea that things have to get worse before they get better.

As thousands of children in our child care centers prepare for 2020, I am confident that they will not have to relive the obstacles we have known. Once and for all, they will have joined in putting to bed the abominable stereotypes that clouded our lives and times. How I would enjoy living long enough to revel in such a long-awaited transformation and progress.

My life has been passed in eras when brown faces have been either scarce or absent from corporate boards and from executive suites.

Who knows? My own great-grandchildren may yet occupy high positions among the Fortune 500 companies, with their brass nameplates on mahogany doors reading "President" or "Vice-President." In the glorious future, legislative halls will ring with the new voices of our people. A new generation of Hispanic leaders will hear their Latin beat resounding on the shores of the Potomac.

When my eldest daughter, Margarita, stops by to pick up her grandchildren, she asks how I'm doing and casts an eye of mock disapproval at the countless papers that lay scattered on the ground around me. She sits for a moment to chat, gracious as always.

As we began our conversation, I ask her, "What do you think the future holds for your grandchildren? What still stands in their way?"

She sees the feigned perplexity in my expression. In her characteristic optimism, she again reveals to me her powers of observation. But there is no way she could hide from me the emotional commitment of her answer: "Daddy, this is Sunday and it's really a bit too late in the afternoon to express how strongly I feel about so many issues. However, there are still two especially disturbing obstacles. More Mexican Americans who have it made still need to speak out, get involved and put their money behind our cause." Then she adds a feisty comment of ominous implications: "Mexico herself must make significant progress against the corruption which has kept her people impoverished for so many centuries. She must awaken to the need for better job opportunities and eliminate shamefully substandard wages, Mexican Americans will continue to bear the economic consequences of mass migration across our southern border."

At one point, Margarita recalled that she once suggested to a corporate vice-president, who had recently moved his business to Mexico, that one way to discourage northward migration would be that large corporations pay at least minimum United States wages. "He refused to debate the issue with me," she said.

On the issue of money, which Margarita raised, I said, "I have spent a lifetime figuring out how to raise money to help our needy. How true it is that our Mexican American community has yet to learn how to give. I have striven through the years to make clear what cause-oriented personal sacrifice is all about. I find it more obvious every day that too few people cheerfully give up Saturdays, Sundays and evenings with family to serve others. I share with my colleagues the difficulty of finding our own people ready to dole out big bucks to charitable causes on a regular basis. I look to the day when millions will be contributed to Mexican American organizations by Mexican American businessmen and civic leaders. One has only to look at the science of fund-raising as practiced by the Jewish community to realize the potential of self-help. Margarita is right on target.

And then there is Mexico. In attempting to fathom the dimensions of what amounts to a bi-national crisis, I have, every year for twenty years, led a delegation of Mexican American leaders to Mexico to seek a commonality of viewpoints. I have lived fully aware that for too long we have not really exchanged dialogue with the Mexican people themselves and that many Mexican Americans look down upon Mexicans as foreigners. However finally in my old age, I am encouraged to see the first signs of real brotherly communication.

As Margarita takes the children and leaves, I feel a sense of affirmation that my daughter and I have come to such broad agreement on what the future holds for our children. How satisfying it is to me, as a father, to realize that my daughter has comprehended my innermost feelings about my life in two cultures. She fully understands how I have always been driven to be involved in direct service to our people. In her world view, even in her personal appearance, she has been described as a carbon copy of her father. How fortunate we are that we have so many bright stars of Margarita's generation to carry on.

As I look back through eight decades of life in two cultures, I have concluded that our Mexican heritage will neither disappear nor fade, but will flourish to illuminate the upward path of countless generations to come.

Now the children and their grandmother are gone. Again, I am alone with my thoughts. In the quiet of the advancing twilight, I close my eyes and see again the sun-drenched hills of Moorpark. A visitor to this tranquil scene of the nineties could hardly imagine the ruthlessness of the local bigotry that raged during Moorpark's bygone days.

But reminiscence casts a golden glow upon childhood memories.

High among my most indelible memories, my wondrous Tarascan kite still soars in triumph against the shoreless blue!